How
We
Lost
the
Vietnam
War

Praise for *How We Lost the Vietnam War*

"A warning for the future." —*CBS Radio*

"Well worth reading. . . . Chilling." —*Library Journal*

"*How We Lost the Vietnam War* will reopen the eyes of many who forgot that Vietnam was a civil war. Ky's reminder that he himself was brought up to regard Ho Chi Minh as a patriot will astonish many. . . . It deserves a wide audience among Americans who were puzzled by much reporting from Saigon." —*Newhouse News Service*

"Ky's book is the first by a major South Vietnamese figure. . . . Interesting." —*Publishers Weekly*

"Ky's account does much to explain the debacle of U.S. involvement in that conflict." —*Best Sellers*

NGUYEN CAO KY

Former Prime Minister of South Vietnam

How
We
Lost
the
Vietnam
War

Cooper Square Press

First Cooper Square Press edition 2002

This Cooper Square Press paperback edition of *How We Lost the Vietnam War* (originally published in Briarcliff Manor, New York in 1976 as *Twenty Years and Twenty Days*, and reprinted in 1976 as a mass-market paperback with its present title) is a retitled unabridged republication of the edition first published in New York in 1976, with the addition of twelve photos. It is reprinted by arrangement with the author.

Designed by David Miller

Published by Cooper Square Press
A Member of the Rowman & Littlefield Publishing Group
200 Park Avenue South, Suite 1109
New York, New York 10003-1503
www.coopersquarepress.com

Distributed by National Book Network

Library of Congress Cataloging-in-Publication Data Available

0-8154-1222-3 (paper : alk. paper)

☉™ The paper used in this publication meets the minimum requirements of American National Standard for Information Sciences—Permanence of Paper for Printed Library Materials, ANSI/NISO Z39.48–1992.
Manufactured in the United States of America.

CONTENTS

1

A QUESTION OF HONOR:

"I'm sorry, the answer is 'No'"

I knew it was the end from the way the Americans refused to look me in the eyes. We were at my house on Tan Son Nhut, the Saigon air base, a few miles outside the city. Though I was now a civilian I still held the rank of marshal in the air force, and was still entitled to my "married quarters." I was sitting there now, on the evening of April 27, 1975, facing Erich Von Marbod, an Assistant Secretary from the Defense Department, and two military advisers called, I think, Stevenson and Smith.

The room was plainly furnished with comfortable armchairs and tables. Its windows looked out across the busy acres of the base from which I had flown hundreds of sorties against the enemy. It was hot. The open windows did nothing to muffle the occasional mortar fire and the heavier boom of artillery, punctuated from time to time by the clang of bells or the wailing of sirens from an ambulance or fire engine.

The dark sky was stained a blotchy red, like a bad painting of a sunset. But the sun had long since gone down, in more ways than one, for the red blotches came from fires ringing the outskirts of Saigon, funeral pyres for South Vietnam, for a cause lost, for a war lost by the world's greatest nation and its smaller comrade in arms.

Even at that moment, looking out of the window, I clung obstinately to a last fragile hope that somehow honor could be salvaged from the holocaust, that I could, metaphorically speaking, dart into the fire and drag that honor out, as one saves a prized battle flag. For weeks I had been trying to persuade the Americans to get rid of President Thieu and then back me in a last-ditch stand which, even if it did not bring victory, might at least give us the chance to argue the eventual peace terms from a position of some strength.

That was why Von Marbod was in my house. Graham Martin, the American ambassador, had already sat in the same chair, as cold and smooth as the marble slab in a mortuary.

A servant poured out more green tea and some Napoleon brandy. There was only one bottle left in the house. Then I turned to Von Marbod and said, "You know my plans. You know that I have explained to Mr. Martin how we could fight on in the Mekong Delta. I know I can organize resistance and hold out perhaps for a few last months. Will the American government support us? Not in men, but with arms. That's all we ask."

The silence never seemed to end. Then it was shattered by just one short sentence. "I'm sorry," said Von Marbod, "the answer is 'No.' "

He spoke in a flat, toneless voice, staring away from me. I wondered what the voice, devoid of any inflection, meant. Despair? Resignation? Or was it shame?

Von Marbod looked up and said quietly, "When I leave Vietnam, Marshal, you will come with me." Then he added with typical generosity, "Better get your family out right away. And don't worry. If worse comes to worst you can come and live in America."

My role in the war had been long, hard, and varied. Starting as a platoon leader in the jungle, I became a pilot, commander of the air force, then prime minister and vice president of my country, and finally, for the last three years, a civilian.

Yet I was never quite a civilian, and as the final tragedy of Vietnam started to unfold early in 1975, I found myself spending less time at my jungle farm, and more and more time at the base, surrounded by politicians and military officers, all of them coming to beg me to help.

And it seems to me that the end is the right place to begin. For even to this day I believe, without vanity, that I could have helped to write a different final chapter from the one I have to write at the end of this tragic story.

Perhaps the United States could never have won the war. But even if one cannot achieve victory, the alternative is not necessarily the humiliation of abject surrender.

To the victor go the spoils. But to the vanquished there can still be honor. As Von Marbod walked out to the jeep and set off along the shell-pocked road to the American embassy I knew that even that was now denied to us.

2

INTO BATTLE:

The reason why

One of the basic defects in America's generous but sometimes misguided role in Vietnam was best summed up by the proverb, "A little learning is a dangerous thing." The American officers and aid teams who came to Vietnam ready and willing to help were rarely able to get under the skin of our people, simply because the surface knowledge they had acquired in a quick training program a few weeks before embarkation went, in fact, only skin deep.

How many of the strapping twenty-year-olds who fought in our country in the late sixties realized that the Americans of a generation before had been helping the French maintain colonial control of our country? How many Americans in Vietnam could really understand that to all of us Ho Chi Minh was, until 1946, a great patriot? As a schoolboy I happily joined in the chanting of a chorus, "No one loves Ho Chi Minh more than the children." And though I became prime minister of my country, dedicated to the overthrow of the Communists, how many Americans could have reconciled my patriotism with the bizarre fact that from time to time my father had, in the early days, helped to supply Ho Chi Minh with ammunition?

To many Americans in Vietnam we were just vaguely "Chinese." We are not. We are Vietnamese. The Americans did not realize that though the first Chinese warlord marched into our Red River Delta in 200 B.C. and the Chinese stayed for ten centuries, we, almost alone in Asia, defeated them, when the Viets, as we were then called, beat the soldiers of the T'ang dynasty and a century later defeated the troops of the Sung

11

dynasty. By the seventeenth century, Vietnam, which means "Land of the South," was no longer a small country, facing its archenemy in the north, but had extended its frontiers until our people looked over the Gulf of Siam.

It is easy to say that none of this matters, but it does; it helps one to understand the reason why. *Why* a villager in the South might hide a killer from the North; *why* "Uncle Ho" could inspire his men while so many of our leaders failed.

I can remember, as though it were yesterday, my father sitting next to me in our house—not far from Ho Chi Minh's headquarters—and forcing me to read a history book he had brought home, telling me, "The past is the key to what you are doing today."

History will help answer the question: "What went wrong?" Two nations lost the war in Vietnam. Now, as I try to analyze the causes leading to that defeat, I must stand them against history where our alliance can be seen in true perspective: on the one hand a country that lives in the past and abhors all change; on the other hand a country that would be lost without a future, without a goal to achieve. We went to war side by side, puzzled by each other, a country of yesterday and a country of tomorrow, each trying to keep in step with the other.

America has the advantage of waging wars from a distance. I have lived almost all my life against a background of machine-gun fire and the crump of bombs. I had my first experience of air raids—by American aircraft—when I was a schoolboy during World War II, living in what would later be called North Vietnam. I was born and raised in the North, in Son Tay, a town of not more than 50,000 people, twenty-five miles northwest of Hanoi. I was born there on September 8, 1930. Years later, in 1970, Son Tay was to come into the news when President Nixon sent commandos to rescue some American airmen being held there. By the time the commandos reached the prison camp it was empty. I told Nixon later, "If I had known you were planning this attack I would have gone along because I know the area like the back of my hand."

Of course it was not North Vietnam when I was a boy. It

was Tonkin. The French, who completed their slow conquest of Indochina in the 1880s, divided it into five colonial territories —Cambodia and Laos, Tonkin, Annam, and Cochin China, the last three together comprising Vietnam.

The capital of Tonkin was Hanoi. Annam, the central and most heavily populated part of Vietnam, was governed from Hue. Cochin China, the southern part of Vietnam, and the most French-influenced, had Saigon as its capital.

I grew up hating the French. They had come originally to Indochina as missionaries in the seventeenth century. Over the years they had made fortunes from the country's rice, rubber, and opium, but they had given back little in return. By exorbitant taxes they had driven our happy peasants to sell their small holdings and work for wages in French factories or on French plantations. They had done virtually nothing to prepare Vietnam for eventual independence, and the illiteracy rate was appalling.

My own family avoided contact with the French as far as possible. My forebears—my grandfather, my father, my uncles —belonged to what was known as the mandarin class—a term that was a legacy of the years of Chinese influence. The mandarins were the scholars and administrators. My father taught Vietnamese pupils in a private school and we also farmed, raising mostly rice and vegetables.

We loved the North, which is as different from the South as New Orleans is different from Detroit, as Naples is from Milan. The North, with its mountains and extinct volcanoes, is in direct contrast to the rich lands of the Mekong Delta. Over the centuries North and South tended to become "separate," speaking with different accents. As in Italy, the Northerners always worked harder than the Southerners, who could relax under a benevolent sun.

In the last years of his life, my father liked to go hunting— everything from elephants to crocodiles—in country near the Chinese frontier. At least that is what we were always told as boys at home. In fact in 1944 and 1945 my father acted from time to time as liaison between guerrilla forces fighting the Japanese and the city dwellers in Son Tay and Hanoi. For my father's happy hunting grounds (and he was a very good hunter) happened to be the area in which Ho Chi Minh was establishing the bases from which he would launch his campaign to rule Vietnam. At that time he was not yet known as Ho. He had been born in Annam as Nguyen Sin Cung but called himself Nguyen Ai Quoc (Nguyen the Patriot) and that was how we all regarded him—as a patriot dedicated to independence for Vietnam.

After traveling the world as a ship's cabin boy and cook, he had been a member of the French Communist Party in the twenties, after which he trained as a professional revolutionary in Moscow, but we did not realize how rabid a Communist he was.

During World War II I went to school in Son Tay and later in Hanoi, but none of us spent much time in school; we kept moving around to avoid American bombers attacking the Japanese who occupied the country. After the defeat of the French in Europe the Japanese had virtually walked into Vietnam where they established a puppet regime of Vichy Frenchmen. Ho led attacks against the Japanese and with other Vietnamese nationalists—not all of them Communists—in May 1941 he organized the Vietminh, a contraction of Vietnam Doc Lap Dong Minh, the League for the Independence of Vietnam.

It is strange, looking back, to think that but for the vigilance of a Japanese soldier, I might today have been a follower of Ho Chi Minh, for as a boy of twelve I was such a little patriot that I ran away from home with a friend to try to join his forces. We saved up a little money, packed a few clothes and all the food we could carry, and set off for the mountains and jungle to the north—the area where my father worked as liaison with the resistance forces. It happened that a Japanese camp had been established near our property in Son Tay and when we "went missing" my mother told the Japanese commander, who telegraphed his outposts to watch out for us. After several days, two extremely dirty and tired boys were found hiding in a ditch, and taken back home. We were only five miles from Ho's headquarters. The Japanese commander in Son Tay was not a bad sort, and I always remember that, as he returned me to our home, he said, "You are a very naughty boy. You made your mother cry." Had we not been discovered that day, my entire life would have been lived differently.

Ho fought his guerrilla war against the Japanese from a base established in China and the wild country of northern Vietnam. In 1942, while shuttling between Vietnam and China, he was caught and thrown into jail by a Chinese warlord and was not released until the next year. This was the moment when he changed his name to Ho Chi Minh, "He Who Shines." Within a year Ho's Vietminh army, commanded by General Vo Nguyen Giap, numbered 10,000.

The atomic bomb at Hiroshima ended World War II in August 1945. The Japanese capitulated. There were still thousands of Japanese in Vietnam but they were no longer in control; nor were the French, driven into China or locked in jails earlier by the Japanese. At this moment the Chinese army was on its way to disarm the Japanese in the North, while the British troops marched into the South.

There was a power vacuum, and Ho filled it. He led his Vietminh troops into Hanoi, and after a few skirmishes with the Japanese, seized power, declaring a provisional Democratic Republic of Vietnam. To the world he proclaimed, "We are convinced that the Allied nations, which at Teheran and San Francisco have acknowledged the principles of self-determination and the equality of nations, will not refuse to acknowledge the independence of Vietnam."

He was very, very wrong, for his "independence" was of the wrong kind.

Ho planned to seize the center and south of Vietnam, of Annam, and of Cochin China. In Annam his plans went well. The thirty-two-year-old Emperor Bao Dai, the Paris-educated pre-war ruler of Annam under the French, had served in the last days of the war as a Japanese puppet. He abdicated, leaving Ho in control.

In Cochin China (South Vietnam) Ho met trouble, in the shape of an advance party of the British Liberation Army. It consisted of only 4,000 men of the 20th Indian division, reinforced by Gurkha battalions. When it arrived in Saigon on September 13, 1945, Ho Chi Minh's men were installed in most government buildings.

The following morning, Vietminh representatives called on the British commander, Major General Douglas Gracey, at Government House, and offered to keep order and disarm the Japanese. Gracey refused to meet them. Instead, he began to turn them out of the government buildings they occupied. He banned demonstrations and public meetings and shut down the Vietnamese press. Then, incredibly, he used Japanese troops to post his proclamation of what amounted to martial law.

Next Gracey opened the jails and released the French prisoners. Twenty-four hours later French troops commanded by Colonel H. J. Cédile, who had parachuted into Cochin China a month earlier, seized the Hôtel de Ville and all government offices not in British hands. By mid-morning the tricolor was flying again in Saigon.

Even as a boy, listening with my father to the clandestine radio, I had believed that the promises of Roosevelt would come true, that when the war ended, Vietnam would be free. I could not have been more wrong.

The overjoyed French began to re-exert their authority. The disgusted Vietnamese hit back with a general strike, cutting power and water supplies. Armed bands of Vietnamese, including the Binh Xuyen, a gangster organization that controlled gambling dens and brothels, went on a rampage. A truce called by the British failed to hold.

When the British left Vietnam in March 1946, the French General Jean Leclerc, the first of many French commanders, set out to reimpose ruthless French control on all Indochina. It was the beginning of a war that would cost the French 174,000 casualties before their defeat at Dien Bien Phu in 1954.

Beaten in World War II, the French were penniless. The Germans had stripped their country bare. The Americans helped in response to French requests for arms to attack Vietnamese—Communists or others—who demanded only freedom. Secretary of State Dean Acheson said that the guns and bombs were to encourage "genuine nationalism."

It is now that one can begin to understand how the Vietminh forces came into their own, and how Ho Chi Minh became a national hero. For as French troops marched north—with plans for a system of phony republics and controlled kingdoms, within a French Union—Ho Chi Minh's resistance mounted. The Vietminh were peasants by day and guerrillas by night. In areas that the French believed were safe, suicide squads of Vietminh struck at French outposts with grenades. There was no safety even in Saigon where restaurant owners erécted wiremesh fences to block grenades thrown from the street by youngsters of my age.

The French brought in their dreaded paratroopers, gradually capturing most of the important cities of northern and central Vietnam, and laying siege to Hanoi and Haiphong, the principal port of the North. Yet never could they establish peace, and it became obvious that no number of military conquests would achieve it.

Emile Bollaert, a veteran Radical Socialist who had become French High Commissioner, tried negotiating with Ho Chi Minh. As a first step, he asked the Emperor Bao Dai, who was living in exile in Hong Kong, to return, hoping we would all rally behind the royal figure. After conferences in Paris in 1949, Bao Dai returned to Hue as the formal head of a new South Vietnamese state.

At the same time, the French started to create a southern Vietnamese military force, to help fight the Vietminh. The Vietminh had now announced its aim: to drive out the French and form a Communist country. That was very different from fighting for freedom, I thought. To counter the help given to Ho Chi Minh by the Russians and the Chinese, the Vietnamese government decided that all youngsters would be drafted. I was about to go to college in 1950, but there was no exemption for students, so I went straight to an officers' training corps and, after six months training, I was commissioned a second lieutenant.

It is curious that, from time to time, people talk about my having served in the French army. I never did. I was *trained* by the French, a very different matter.

As a second lieutenant I was in charge of an all-Vietnamese

platoon of twenty men manning an outpost in the Red River Delta, the northern lowland, and it was here that the battle between Nationalists and Communists really started. The delta was infested with Communist guerrillas, as the Vietminh soldiers had become known, and I suppose I was one of the first Nationalists to go into operation against them.

In addition to supplies from Russia and China, the Vietminh also had large supplies of arms and ammunition left behind by the Japanese, and dropped by Americans to the guerrillas during World War II. But for the new Vietnamese army there were no American weapons. The French vetoed all American aid for us, after General Marcel Carpentier, the French commander in chief, threatened to resign if Dean Acheson's "genuine nationalists" received one bullet or one rifle. "The Vietnamese have no generals, no colonels, and no military organization that could effectively utilize the equipment," said Carpentier, who was either scared or stupid. So all the guns went to the French, who had only one real objective: to regain the mastery of Indochina, one of the richest areas on earth.

I was an army officer for only a few weeks before the French-backed Vietnam government asked for volunteers to form an air force. I leapt at the opportunity and after an examination in Hanoi I was sent for a year of basic training in Marrakesh, Morocco, then still a French colony. I was a born flyer, if I say so myself, and I had no problems making the grade.

Then I went on to France for over two years of advanced training on DC3 transport planes at the Avord air base, south of Paris, and after that to Algeria for five months bombing and strafing training. I graduated as a fully qualified pilot in 1954.

Much had happened in Vietnam while I had been out of the country. In 1950 Ho Chi Minh had acquired military training camps in Yunnan, southern China, and had been elevated by the world's Communists to a place alongside Stalin and Mao Tse-tung in their trinity of leaders. Ho had ruthlessly weeded all non-Communists from the Vietminh, which still controlled most of the northern half of North Vietnam.

Meanwhile the inept general Carpentier had gone, and the more far-sighted General Jean de Lattre de Tassigny was doubling as commander in chief of French forces in Indochina and as High Commissioner, and he *did* allow the Americans to help the Vietnamese army, saying, "This war against Communism is the war of Vietnam for Vietnam, and France will carry it on for you only if you carry it on with her. Young men of Vietnam, the moment has come for you to defend your country." By 1953 there were 60 Vietnamese battalions totaling about 150,000 men.

By the time I arrived back in Vietnam in 1954 the war was over. The peace talks in Geneva resulted in the formal partition of Vietnam at the 17th parallel. Above the line was the Republic of North Vietnam, some 63,360 square miles, and below the line South Vietnam, about 65,726 square miles. The populations were also roughly equal.

The Geneva conference, however, did more than carve two countries out of one. It transferred South Vietnam from a "local" issue to the sphere of global politics. Before Geneva, America, though supplying France with weapons to fight the Vietminh, had kept its distance. After Geneva, America realized that the threat of Communism was more serious in Asia than in Europe. The United States believed itself to be the free world's shield against Communist aggression, and so Indochina became another pawn in the cold war after its "future" was settled by the great powers (the United States, Soviet Russia, France, Britain, and China) at the conference table. By the end of that conference American diplomats were convinced that a stable South Vietnam was vital to world—and American —security, particularly as the new Red China had become increasingly powerful under the five-year-old rule of Mao Tsetung.

To the Americans, the solution seemed simple: make everyone in South Vietnam happy, give everyone all the good things of life, and nobody would become a Communist. Gratefully Vietnamese politicians accepted their plans to build "a strong, free nation."

The Americans even found Ngo Dinh Diem to be a suitable prime minister, an austere, honest bachelor, descended from a line of scholars and advisers to the emperor. Diem had lived in

America for two years after refusing to serve in the Japanese puppet regime. The future, it seemed, must be bright.

Meanwhile, as Ho prepared to enter Hanoi, millions of anti-Communist North Vietnamese were moving south. When I returned I could not at first trace my own large family. They had moved south while I was training in France, though I knew nothing about this. My first job when I returned home as a pilot in the air force was to fly the last refugees out of North Vietnam, so I became one of the last anti-Communists to leave there.

Even after Hanoi had been occupied by the North Vietnamese I managed to make one last flight to Haiphong and spent the evening in a downtown restaurant. I was dining quietly (in my air force uniform) when a man in civilian clothes sat down uninvited at my table and for an hour tried to persuade me to join the Communists. After I had told him "No" several times he began to get aggressive and I decided to cut my dinner short and return to the base quickly.

I lifted my DC3 off the runway that night with relief, and I have never been back to North Vietnam since. From this time on, my home was to be Saigon.

The curtain was about to go up on another war, the war between the Communist-backed North and the American-backed South. This was "my" war, and it fell roughly into two parts.

After the Geneva conference, Ho Chi Minh deliberately left behind in the South a hard-core team of over 5,000 tough guerrillas ready to strike when he ordered them to do so. At first, they concerned themselves mainly with the "political struggle" and the country was relatively quiet. In 1956 Vice President Nixon visited Vietnam to talk with the United States advisers and I remember hearing Nixon say on the radio: "The militant march of Communism has been halted."

In fact it was just starting. At Geneva both sides had agreed to hold free popular elections in both North and South, for the unification of the country. President Diem rightly refused to hold any elections until the people of the North were allowed to vote freely.

This was the spark that set off the shooting war, because the cancellation of the elections robbed Ho Chi Minh of the victory denied to him at Geneva. There was only one way now for him. Force.

The shooting war started with the formation of the National Liberation Front (NLF) in South Vietnam. This was, in my opinion, the most sinister enemy we had to fight in Vietnam, for it was a shadowy opponent within our own country, a ghostly army that lived underground, emerging to fight only at night, but impossible to bring to battle like regular troops. It was also a political force that fought us for the minds of the people.

In December 1960, when American military personnel in Vietnam totaled 900, the NLF produced a ten-point manifesto, pledging among other things to overthrow the "colonial regime of the American imperialists" and President Diem, and to re-establish normal relations between North and South, and the eventual peaceful reunification of the country. Within a year their ranks had swollen to 300,000. They worked in cooperation with Hanoi, on which they depended for supplies. Their military wing, the People's Self Defense Forces, instituted guerrilla raids and sabotage, building up its army by a "growth and split" program. A trained platoon of terrorists would split to provide the nucleus of three platoons. When these three were fully trained they would split again, each providing the nucleus for three more.

When NLF cadres went into villages they wore the black pajamas of peasants. Instead of military ranks they used titles like chairman or secretary. They made a point of addressing villagers by intimate words such as "me" (mother) and "bac" (uncle), emphasizing that they were not foreigners, nor bureaucrats and officials, like the South Vietnamese who visited them. As the American advisers multiplied, the NLF preached against the American "imperialists" and their Vietnamese "lackeys." They played on the theme of exploitation: that the peasant worked all day in the paddy fields or a soldier fought in the trenches while others never seemed to work or fight. Their tactics were often successful.

The original members of the NLF, who were mostly peasants, were joined by tradesmen; they were not all Communists, though recruits found that if they wanted to progress in the organization the key was membership in the Party. Until the end of the war, the North Vietnamese took the greatest care never to confuse the NLF with the Viet Cong—the term invented by Diem to describe anyone actively fighting South Vietnam. Viet Cong stood for Vietnamese Communist, and was deliberately intended to blanket the Northern guerrillas with the National Liberation Front and any other factions linked with Hanoi.

The North Vietnamese, however, claimed that the NLF was not exclusively Communist, but a nationalist organization, and always referred to their troops as the People's Liberation Army, never using the term Viet Cong.

No wonder that, as the real fighting war opened up, the North Vietnamese premier, Pham Van Dong, felt strong enough to make one of the most prophetic boasts of the war: "We will drive the Americans into the sea."

3

AIRBORNE:

I work with Colby of the CIA

Flying in the fifties was magnificently exciting. With every day that passed, I loved the air more and more. We were all young, a team trained and working together.

In those days flying really meant something; it still held some of the excitement that had made flying such a thrill in World War II, for in Vietnam a man was on his own when he sat in a plane—mostly old DC3s. Often I had no navigational aids. Individuality counted. I was not just the "chauffeur" of a large aircraft with automatic equipment to help me. We flew with our noses, amid dangers magnified by sudden tropical storms and hurricanes, and often without knowing exactly where the nearest airfield was. We could not fly at 50,000 feet like today's pilots. We rarely had people sitting in control towers telling us what route to fly, or at what height or speed.

The Vietnamese air force was engaged mostly in transport—hauling men and machines, often to lonely outposts, putting our planes down on makeshift airfields—until a dramatic change occurred in 1960. By then I was commander of the air base just outside Saigon. I was thirty. Promotion had been swift in a service that was small. The commander of the air force sent for me unexpectedly. "We've been working on new plans with the American CIA," he said, "to drop specially trained agents into key positions in North Vietnam. The CIA is training the men, and helping to choose the targets from information they have received. What we need now from you is a highly trained group of flyers to drop the right men at the right spot."

He must have seen my look of excitement, for he warned me, "It won't be easy. You'll have to hedge-hop at zero feet, to fly under enemy radar. You'll have no navigational aids. And," he added, a trifle dryly, "the C-47 [the military term for the DC3] isn't exactly the world's most up-to-date and maneuverable plane."

"When do we start?" I asked.

The hazards were obvious. I decided that nobody should be compelled to undertake this kind of mission and I called for volunteers among the seventy or eighty pilots in my wing. Every man stepped forward.

Within two days we started intensive training, learning to fly on moonlit nights ten to fifteen feet above ground. I devised a scheme of "double navigation," taking two navigators on each trip. One concentrated on navigating us to the target, the other on giving the pilot a visual ground fix every two minutes. We learned to study every detail of the terrain days before we set off, so that, aided by moonlight, the visual navigator could read the ground rushing past us below as easily as a map.

While I was training the crews, the CIA were training the men we would drop in undercover work, demolition, and radio transmission. Already the Americans had a military command in Saigon, though at that time they were in the country in a purely advisory capacity. They had taken the place of the French in helping us. The CIA group training the parachutists was part of this command. As the training reached its climax we finally met.

I returned to the hangar after one night flight to find a stranger waiting to meet me. He wore glasses, was rather slight and pale, with nondescript hair. He spoke very softly and seemed a quiet man. I remember thinking he looked like a student of philosophy, until I saw the eyes behind the glasses: never still, watching every movement, watching everybody in the room.

He announced his name, which meant nothing to me: William E. Colby. It was my first contact with the CIA and it was a curious situation, for in a way we were working along parallel lines: while Colby trained the parachutists, I trained the pilots. Neither had anything to do with the other, for the training was obviously totally different. I make the point because several American newspapers later accused me of working for the CIA. It was a ridiculous assertion, based no doubt on the fact that I did see a great deal of Colby after our first meeting.

But I never worked for the CIA. Indeed, the CIA worked for us, for the CIA was not only training men who would be dropped, but was also providing vital information from North Vietnam, and consequently often chose the places where agents would be dropped above the 17th parallel.

Colby seemed worried, and I soon discovered why. Like any topflight intelligence agent he was deeply concerned with security. Now, as the time approached when the training would end and we would go into action, rumors were spreading about the twenty or so pilots who always dressed in black flying suits (that was my idea) and who seemed to fly off into the night on strange missions which were never publicized.

"If the rumors increase," said Colby, "there'll be a leak to North Vietnam, and then we might as well call the whole deal off."

He made an unwelcome proposal: all of us on special training should share a villa inside the base area, and never leave it except to go to the hangars. We had to agree, but it was like being in a prison. The only view out of our front door was the back of a Vietnamese sentry. We missed the Officers' Club with its billiard table and bar. Finally I told Colby, "At least let my boys have the run of the base." He started to protest, but I rushed on, "It's all very well for you, but you don't realize how hard it is to keep up morale among men training to fly to targets they don't know, to drop men they often don't know. Morale has gone to hell; they must have a chance to let off steam."

Colby saw the point, and though we still lived in the villa under strict guard we were allowed the equivalent of an American navy "Happy Hour" in the club from time to time.

Colby had one other security idea—a good one. As the training ended, we left our air force planes in the hangar and started to use similar Vietnamese civil air transport planes boldly painted with their trademark Air VIAT. To any prying eyes it appeared that we were just helping out the hard-pressed civilian authorities.

The night of the first operational flight approached. The crews spent a week studying every centimeter of the route to the drop zone. Before we left each crew member and each parachutist was given $100 so that if we had to make a forced landing outside Vietnam we could survive. (This money was returned at the end of each trip.)

We were airborne about 9 P.M. on a bright moonlit night and reached the drop zone about 1:30 A.M. with no problems, landing back in Saigon about six in the morning.

As I clambered out, stiff and tired, I said to my navigator, "What I wouldn't give for a bottle of ice-cold champagne."

Colby must have been a mind reader. There he was in the hangar waiting for us, beaming with delight at the success of our first mission—and ready to prove it with a case of champagne.

We had our problems during the two years I led the team on this kind of work. We lost two planes, and on one occasion I had almost reached the drop zone when engine trouble developed and I had to turn back, and was lucky to land in South Vietnam. This sort of mishap meant frustrating delay as we could fly only on moonlit nights—perhaps three a month at the most.

When things went wrong I sometimes wondered whether Colby thought we young pilots were exaggerating our prowess at low flying, and that maybe a plane was missing because it was flying too high—even fifty feet—and had been picked up by enemy radar. After all, it is not easy to assess men's characters when social contact is entirely absent. For the CIA and the pilots never mixed, never even met off limits. Our only contacts were in the hangar or the Officers' Club. There was no fraternization. I think it was a pity in many ways, for you can learn a lot about a man if you visit his house, become his friend.

However, I did have the opportunity of proving to Colby that I had not been exaggerating. It came when I was asked to fly him and a party of Americans to Danang on the coast. Before setting off across the sea I said, "Now, Mr. Colby, you have asked us to go in for low flying. I'm going to show you how good we are at it."

I flew out over the sea at zero feet—and I mean zero. After ten minutes I looked back at Colby and his friends. Colby's face had turned almost yellow as we skimmed five feet above the waves. Not until we landed at Danang did he give a faint smile. Then, as we walked to the hangar, his face became a little pinker, and he turned to me. All he said was, "Ky, the next time you fly me like that so close to the water, let me know beforehand and I'll bring my fishing rod."

While we were getting on with our job of fighting the war, the first ominous cracks in South Vietnam's flimsy political structure appeared. After nearly five years in office, President Diem had let power go to his head and criticism of his regime was growing. In April 1960, eighteen prominent Vietnamese, including ten former ministers, held a press conference for American journalists at the Hotel Caravelle. There they denounced Diem for driving the peasants into the arms of the Communists and called for an end to censorship and detention without trial.

Like many of us, they were concerned at the swift increase in the activities of the Viet Cong, numbering about 10,000 by 1960, who posed an almost insoluble problem and were either forcing or cajoling more and more peasants to join their ranks. Diem's forces outnumbered them seven to one, but were powerless to contain the Viet Cong, who could strike where they liked and when they liked.

The eighteen critics demanded that Diem should either liberalize his regime by adopting administrative, economic, and military reforms, or he should step down. For this outspokenness most of them were arrested.

Unfortunately this incident, typifying the growing restlessness of the people, did not prevent President Eisenhower later in the year from sending congratulations to Diem on the fifth anniversary of his accession to power. It was not as though Eisenhower was unaware of the feeling against Diem. He knew perfectly well that Diem was unpopular from his own spy network in Vietnam, which had reported to him the previous August in a special intelligence estimate, "In the absence of more effective government measures to protect the peasants and win their positive cooperation, the prospect is for expansion of the areas of Viet Cong control in the countryside. Dissatisfaction and discontent with the government will probably continue to rise . . . if they remain unchecked, they will almost certainly in time cause the collapse of Diem's regime."

Of course Eisenhower knew that by now Diem had become a recluse, leaving the day-to-day running of government in the hands of his venal brother Ngo Dinh Nhu, who controlled the secret police. The ruthless activities of Nhu, his insatiable greed, the terror tactics of his henchmen, turned many an honest peasant into a Communist. Among other things, Nhu took back much of the land which had earlier been distributed to peasants under Diem's land reform, so that by 1960, 75 percent of the land was owned by 15 percent of the people.

Diem had also angered the peasants by breaking the centuries-old tradition that villages were autonomous, that their affairs were run by their own freely elected leaders. He had replaced all local village chiefs and councils with his own handpicked "professional" provincial chiefs. It is not difficult to see the hand of Nhu behind this break with village tradition. Indeed, Nhu, with his secret police and informers, was as valuable to Ho Chi Minh as if he had been on his payroll. Yet here was Eisenhower going out of his way to assure Diem of his faith in him, and promising continued American assistance.

Something had to explode, and three weeks later it did. An army unit attempted to overthrow Diem—and in the process took me captive. The coup was led by Colonel Nguyen Chanh Thi of the paratroopers, whose camp adjoined the air force base that I commanded. Early on the morning of November 11, 1960, his three paratroop battalions seized most of the key points in Saigon, including the air base, which made me their prisoner. Then they prepared to launch an attack on the president's palace.

It was then that Thi made a fatal error. When Diem offered to bargain with him, Thi agreed. The initial attack was never followed up, for Diem promised Thi on the evening of the same day that he would resign and allow Thi to form a government of "national union." To Thi, this seemed to be total victory and the next morning Thi broadcast his plans from the radio station, which was in his hands.

At the same time Diem—no doubt inspired by the wily Nhu —was quietly moving loyal troops into the capital from the North and South. Almost before Thi realized what was happening, Diem's forces had recaptured many of the key positions in Saigon. The coup collapsed.

The first I knew about it was when Thi and his fellow plotters roared up to the air base, which was technically in their hands. Thi looked terrified and blurted out to me, "Ky, we have failed! We must get out quickly or Diem will have our heads." He begged for an aircraft to take them to the safety of Cambodia.

I wanted to help them. The paratroopers and the air force had always been very close because of the nature of their work. Yet I could hardly fly them out myself, for if I did I would never have been able to return to Vietnam.

Then I discovered a way out. One of the plotters was an air force pilot who was a distant relation to Thi. After some hesitation, I "gave" him a DC3, and fifteen of the plotters made their getaway. Of course, I never got the plane back and Diem was suspicious. His military security officers sent for me and demanded to know how the plotters had obtained the aircraft.

I explained that they had been fully armed and in control of the base and I had been forced to hand the plane over. They believed me; at least, no action was taken against me and I carried on as commander of the base. Diem carried on as president, promising reforms, but in fact merely retiring into the background again and allowing Nhu to strengthen his autocratic rule.

In February 1962 two dissident air force officers bombed and strafed the palace in an attempt to kill Diem, but though they destroyed one wing, none of the Diem family was hurt.

Criticism of Diem began to grow in the American press as well as at home, and another coup was planned. In this one I was to be more actively involved.

4

DIEM:

The CIA backs our coup

For months Saigon had heard rumors of an American-backed coup to oust President Ngo Dinh Diem. It was planned by Lieutenant General Duong Van Minh, a burly man known to all as Big Minh, in order to distinguish him from General Tran Van Minh. Almost at the last moment I became involved, after what, to Western eyes, must seem an extraordinary prologue: a visit to a fortune-teller.

My feelings about Diem were well known. In the 1954 election I shared with many thousands the fervent hope that this devoutly religious man would prove to be the savior of our country. Like all my family, I helped to vote Diem into power.

I remember the awe with which Diem was regarded in the days after his election, particularly in the United States. When he visited Washington in 1957, to address a joint session of Congress, he traveled in the presidential plane and Eisenhower was at the airport to meet him. Back home, we read the *Life* magazine profile of a "tough miracle man." Mayor Robert Wagner of New York described him as "a man history may judge as one of the great figures of the twentieth century." And even as late as 1961, Vice President Johnson, when visiting in Saigon, called him "the Winston Churchill of Asia."

But power, even if it does not always corrupt, often blinds people, changes their ideas, their hopes, and leads to frustration among their followers. This was particularly true among the young officers like myself who thirsted for only one thing: victory over the Communists who were tearing our lives and our country apart.

31

Diem was a bachelor who had taken a vow of chastity. He lived an almost priestlike life, each day becoming more and more isolated from his people. He was a rigid authoritarian, and such a stickler for protocol that no cabinet minister dared turn his back on him; after Diem terminated an interview, the cabinet minister would always walk backward out of the room. True, this was all part of an archaic code in Vietnamese court circles that had applied throughout the ages, but now it was out of place.

Diem had his ideals, and was at heart an honest man, but he became a dupe for others. I did not realize it at the time, but looking back now after having been in power myself, I can see the traps into which he fell. In the first months of power, a man must personally examine the good things he wants to do for his country. Inevitably he becomes surrounded by advisers he needs, experts in fields where he needs specialized help. If a leader is clever enough to find good advisers, then he can tread a clean and honest path. But most of the time—and in most cases—a leader tends to be surrounded by either the inefficient or the corrupt. Toward the end, Diem felt he was a man of God sent down to save Vietnam, that he could leave everything to his advisers.

In Diem's case, his chief political adviser, and head of the secret police, was not only cruel and corrupt, but happened to be his brother, who in turn was married to an equally venal and wicked woman. Ngo Dinh Nhu was born in 1911 near Hue, one of five sons of this distinguished Catholic family, and soon became known as the "Oriental Richelieu" of South Vietnam. While Diem was a roly-poly man, reminding one writer of a polished statue of the Buddha, Nhu was thin, fierce-looking, and hungry for power. His wife, Tran Le Xuan Nhu, was born a Buddhist and converted to Catholicism when she married Nhu at the age of eighteen. Since President Diem was a bachelor, the imperious, beautiful, intolerant Madame Nhu became in effect First Lady of South Vietnam. Her name, translated, means "Tears of Spring." Behind her back she was called Lucrezia Borgia.

I first met Madame Nhu in an elevator on my way to a party

given by the American air attaché. She was with an American officer and I was fascinated by the way she talked to him. I had never heard any Vietnamese woman behave in public as she did, and while I was waiting for a drink, I pointed her out to a friend and asked, "Who on earth is that horrible woman?"

"Don't you know?" he replied, "that's Madame Nhu."

I am sure I would have been jailed if I had not had one or two good friends in Nhu's police force, because every member of the air force under my command was watched and reported on. His spies were everywhere. Every time any of us went into Saigon for dinner or to a party, our movements were reported to Nhu. He knew everyone we met. He was very well organized. What a tragedy that he did not harness his talents against the Communists. He would have rendered a great service to his country.

Instead, in the end, Nhu and his nationwide secret police had more influence on the government and the country than Diem himself, simply because the Nhus deliberately encouraged Diem's priestlike isolation. He had no idea how he was being manipulated.

I remember one day going down to the colorful, bustling market in Saigon. The vendors were more excited than usual, because President Diem had decided to visit the market so that he could, as he put it, "keep in touch with the people." How little he knew *how* to keep in touch with the people. The previous day Nhu's henchmen had visited every stall on the president's route and warned each shopkeeper to cut prices in half if the president asked them how much rice or mangoes or anything else cost. Diem merely wanted to see for himself that prices were stable—at a time when prices in Saigon were skyrocketing—and he blissfully expressed his pleasure at the price stability in the Saigon market. Prices were doubled the moment he returned to the president's palace.

Because Nhu was corrupt, Diem had to be shielded more and more from the truth. Even when Diem initiated good plans, they got stuck in the pipeline because Nhu was getting a rake-off. For instance, when Diem helped to start kibbutz-style villages capable of defending themselves—in the same way as the Home Guard villages had been used to combat Communism in Malaya—somehow the arms Diem promised a village failed to materialize. Nhu's men had been to the arms depot first, and guns that should have been issued free had to be bought on the black market.

Yet the kibbutz villages had to *look* successful, if only to prevent Diem from asking awkward questions. Nhu went to almost ludicrous lengths to hide the facts from his brother. I remember the time Diem visited one village which had been started less than a year previously, Nhu's men dug up a grove of orange trees laden with fruit from a neighboring, long-established village, transplanted them for one afternoon, and after Diem had gone, dug them up and returned them to their rightful owners.

Something had to be done. Yet nothing was, largely because the Diem regime had been solidly bolstered by the Americans for eight years. But in 1963 Diem—or, rather, Nhu—went too far, and the Americans saw the writing on the wall, and decided that Diem must go. They could do nothing themselves, but they did give tacit approval to a group of generals plotting a coup.

What led to this change of heart was the age-old problem of the Buddhist quest for political power. Roughly eleven million of the country's fifteen million people were Buddhists but only about one in four of them—about four million—were practicing followers of the Buddha. As a Catholic who at one time had been intended for the priesthood, Diem had spent much of his time in Catholic retreats in the United States before his return to government in Vietnam. The million Catholic refugees who crossed the 17th parallel from North Vietnam at the time of partition were among his strongest supporters. They established themselves in Catholic communities, principally in central Vietnam, which was also the stronghold of Buddhism. Soon the Buddhists became envious, claiming that the newly arrived Catholics were being allotted the most fertile land and receiving the biggest grants for schools and hospitals.

The friction between Buddhists and Catholics came to a head in 1963 in Hue, traditional seat of Buddhism in Vietnam, when rival celebrations clashed. The Buddhists were celebrating the anniversary of the Buddha's birth; the Catholics were commemorating the anniversary of the consecration of the Archbishop of Hue. The Catholics were allowed to fly the Vatican flag and parade sacred objects; the Buddhists were refused permission to do the same.

On May 8, the Buddha's birthday, Buddhists converged outside the radio station in Hue. When ordered to disperse they refused. Fire hoses and tear gas failed to drive them away. On Nhu's orders Major Dang Sy, deputy chief of the province and a Catholic, ordered live ammunition and grenades to be issued. Nine Buddhists died, killed by Sy's forces according to the Buddhist leaders, by Communist grenades according to Nhu.

The fuse was lit. In Saigon a saffron-robed priest had himself soaked in gasoline and then committed sacrificial suicide by fire at a busy road junction. Six more were to follow his example. The dramatic newsreel and press pictures went around the world and the world was horrified. Students in Saigon and Hue, not notably militant before, took to the streets in demonstrations. Diem acceded to certain Buddhist demands, including their right to fly flags, but Nhu called him a coward for these concessions.

It was at this moment that Madame Nhu uttered the words that made her one of the most despised women of our age, when she cried, "I would clap my hands at seeing another monk barbecue show."

According to Nhu, the Buddhists were merely seeking publicity and were influenced by Communists. Dying for a cause did not make it just, he declared, and determined to teach the Buddhists a lesson. On August 21, 1963, he acted ferociously. Using white-uniformed Special Forces and combat police—largely paid for by American money—he stormed the Xa Loi and other venerated Buddhist pagodas throughout the country. In all, 1,400 men, mostly monks, were dragged to jails where they were beaten, half starved, sometimes subjected to electric shock torture. The American embassy was horrified, and taken completely by surprise. This was no accident. To make sure the Americans could not interfere during the long hours of the night, Nhu's men cut all the phone wires to the embassy.

That was the night of the pagodas. The following evening Henry Cabot Lodge arrived as American ambassador, succeeding Ambassador Frederick Nolting. That was the week when finally the Americans decided to get rid of their protégé, not by ordering Diem out of office, which would smack of colonialism (and would have outraged the Vietnamese) but by the simpler method of backing a group of generals who had long been planning a coup.

Led by Big Minh, who was military adviser to Diem, the generals included General Tran Van Don, acting chief of the Joint General Staff, General Tran Thien Khiem, the JGS executive officer, General Nguyen Khanh, commander of Second Corps, north of Saigon, and General Nguyen Van Thieu, commanding the 5th Division, which was stationed north of the capital.

Before taking any irrevocable step, Lodge did try to persuade Diem to get rid of Nhu, and form a more liberal government. John Richardson, the CIA chief in Saigon, specifically warned Washington that Saigon was "an armed camp" and that the Nhu family were digging in for "a last-ditch battle." However, it seemed impossible to change Diem's rigid stance, or his mistaken loyalty to his brother.

When Lodge begged Diem to release some of the arrested Buddhists and student demonstrators in order not to exacerbate public (and American) opinion further, he asked him, "Isn't there some *one* thing you may think of that is within your capabilities to do, Mr. President, that would favorably impress U.S. opinion?" According to the ambassador, "Diem gave me a blank look and changed the subject."

So the American ambassador authorized the CIA to help the generals with "tactical planning." Colonel Lucien Conein, a CIA agent, met quickly with Big Minh, and before long the CIA was providing Big Minh with details of armaments kept at Camp Longthanh, a secret base of Special Forces loyal to Nhu. Meanwhile President Kennedy apparently indicated that Lodge had his full support and that he would do everything necessary to help conclude the operation successfully.

It was now that I came into the picture. I knew a great deal —though no details, of course—of what was going on. Common sense alone made it obvious that the present turmoil could not continue much longer. But I was intrigued by one factor. Though I knew that most of the top generals were in favor of a coup, I knew also that the Saigon troops would certainly be loyal to Diem, and so would those in the Mekong Delta, who I was certain, would not hesitate to march northward if ordered to do so.

I was thinking along these lines in my office at the Saigon air base when I received a telephone call from Colonel Do Mau, the chief of military security, who was in close contact with the president. He asked me if I would see him at his office. When I arrived, his first question was, "Ky, I know a very good fortune-teller. Would you like to go and have your fortune told?"

"But I've never been to a fortune-teller in my life," I replied.

"Never mind, there's always a first time."

In fact, I was not surprised by his insistence, for Colonel Do Mau was obsessed by fortune-telling. Fortune-tellers are very common in the East, and almost everyone patronizes them, but to Colonel Do Mau it was far more than just a popular amusement. He kept horoscopes of all high-ranking officers and many politicians. He would discover the date of a man's birth, the circumstances, and then have the man's horoscope cast.

We set off in a taxi to the back streets of Saigon, ending up before a door in a shabby street. An old man ushered us into a dingy room lined with books, scrolls, astronomy charts, maps. Do Mau gave him the details of my birth, and then asked him two questions.

The first was: "Is this man honest, someone I can trust, who will never betray me or other people?"

The old man patiently studied his books, looked up and replied, "Yes, you can trust him."

Then Do Mau asked his second question: "Does this man's star foretell that he will one day go to jail?"

Once again the fortune-teller pored over his charts and books until he decided, "No, this man will never go to jail as long as he lives."

We returned to Do Mau's office and when I sat down opposite him, on the other side of his desk, he told me without preamble, "Some of the general officers are preparing a coup against President Diem. I want to know if you are willing to rally with us."

The question was not unexpected, and I never hesitated before replying, "Yes, of course."

"Wait for developments," said Do Mau. I returned to the air base, where I was soon contacted by an army colonel who took me secretly to see General Tran Thien Khiem, executive officer of the Joint General Staff. The colonel and I set off alone in a civilian car which bore no military markings, took a roundabout route, and finally left the car and walked the last quarter of a mile to Khiem's house.

Khiem had taken care to be alone with me. "We know the air base commander is a close friend of Nhu's," he said, "but you are in command of a wing. I just want to be completely reassured that if necessary we can depend on you to help us—*actively.*" He stressed the last word. "We will let you know the time and date."

The coup, in fact, was postponed several times, and when it did take place I knew nothing at first. I was having lunch in a Saigon restaurant when I heard the squeal of brakes. My driver hurried in and blurted, "Colonel, you'd better return to the base. Something strange is happening." I was out of the restaurant in two minutes and sped the jeep back to base myself. At the gates stood Colonel Mai, chief of staff of the air force.

"Thank God you're here," he cried. "The coup has started, and we want you to arrest Colonel Huynh Huu Hien [the commander of the air force] and prepare crews for a scrambling."

Though I believed that Diem had to go, I did not want to involve my men or brother officers in a coup against their will, so I drove straight to my wing and assembled all the personnel —pilots, navigators, engineers, maintenance staff—in a hangar. There I told them, "There is a coup against President Diem. I am siding with the army. But you don't have to if you don't want to. Those who are against the coup can go home, and I suggest they remain quietly at home until everything has settled down. Those who trust me and want to stay with me, step forward and I will distribute arms to protect the air base."

Every man took one step forward. Assured of their backing, I grabbed a sub-machine gun, and drove to the air commander's office a quarter of a mile away. Colonel Hien was in the inner office. I knocked, walked in alone. He was sitting at his desk. Saluting politely, I said, "Commander, you are under arrest."

He did not seem surprised.

At first all went well, and the coup was launched with military precision. Spearheaded by two marine and two airborne battalions, and backed by thirty tanks, Big Minh's troops had no difficulty in quickly capturing the radio station and central police headquarters, together with the Ministry of Defense and Ministry of Interior—both key offices.

Little blood was spilled. But speed was vital, and after an hour army colleagues phoned me that the tempo of the attack was slowing down. Nhu's loyal troops around the presidential palace were offering stiff resistance, as I had expected. Inside the palace Diem—unaware of the role played by the Americans in backing the coup—telephoned Ambassador Lodge, telling him, "Some units have made a rebellion." He asked for clarification of the American attitude. An embarrassed Mr. Lodge took refuge in pointing out that it was 4:30 A.M. in Washington, and so the State Department would know nothing anyway as the capital was asleep.

Lodge did, however, tell Diem that he was worried about the president's physical safety. Knowing that the Americans had demanded guarantees from Big Minh that no harm befall Diem, Lodge was able to say, "I understand that those in charge of the coup have offered you and your brother safe conduct out of the country if you resign. Have you heard of this?" After a pause Diem replied that he had not, and added, "You have my telephone number."

Just before three o'clock General Khiem telephoned me. I

could sense the urgency in his voice as he said, "Ky, Diem's bodyguards are holding us up—and time is running out. It's now or never. Are you ready to help?"

"Of course, right away." I slammed down the telephone and called for two experienced pilots to scramble. At that time we had no modern fighter planes, only T-28s, but they could carry bombs and rockets.

"Take up a couple of planes," I told them, "and fly right over the top of the presidential palace. Go in low—it's more frightening. Then fire a few rockets on the big army camp next to the palace."

They did just that. After they had fired only two rockets Diem's garrison surrendered. To me that was a historic moment, not only because it turned the balance in the overthrow of the Diem regime, but as a flyer I was experiencing for the first time the value of air power supporting hard-pressed ground troops. I am convinced that if I had never ordered up those two puny planes, the coup would have failed. After that, during the years that followed, air power played a vital role in the war. But for me it all started on that day.

All was now fairly quiet in Saigon, though the sounds of gunfire occasionally echoed near the base. The two planes, their job done, landed safely. Within thirty minutes Khiem's troops had entered the palace and the coup was over.

Two problems still remained. Diem and his hated brother Nhu had fled through an underground tunnel and had, for the moment, vanished. Khiem told me this on the phone, then added a more sinister piece of information. General Huynh Van Cao, in charge of troops in the Mekong Delta, and a former aide of Diem's, was threatening to march north and relieve the city.

"Shall we attack them?" Khiem asked me on the phone.

"I don't think we'll need to do that," I replied. "Let me just warn them first."

I sent only one aircraft down to the Mekong Delta. It carried no bombs or rockets, just a stark warning in the form of a message which the pilot dropped over Cao's headquarters. I wrote it out myself, and it read: "Stay where you are. If there are any suspicious troop movements, the air force will bomb you."

That was enough.

Now only one problem remained. Where were Diem and Nhu? The Americans quickly reminded the plotters that in return for help with the coup, they must take no bloody revenge. As General Paul D. Harkins, chief of the American Military Assistance Command in Saigon, had cabled the Pentagon earlier in the week, "Rightly or wrongly we have backed Diem for eight long, hard years. To me it seems incongruous now to get him down, kick him around, and get rid of him. The United States has been his mother superior and father confessor since he's been in office and he leaned on us heavily."

Because the State Department knew this to be true, it warned the coup leaders, in effect, "No reprisals."

It was not to be. When Diem finally escaped and took refuge in a church in Cholon, the Chinese city-within-a-city on the edge of Saigon, he telephoned General Khiem, knowing from Lodge that he would be protected by safe conduct. Only when he was assured that he would be taken to the airfield did Diem agree on the telephone to surrender. An armored car was sent to collect the two brothers, but once they entered the vehicle both were murdered. A police officer first shot Diem in the head, then he shot Nhu. Though dead, Nhu was stabbed several times by other officers.

Washington did not immediately recognize the new government of Big Minh which they had quietly helped to engineer, but not because of the murders. Apparently Secretary of State Dean Rusk believed that a delay in official recognition of Big Minh would help to stifle possible world criticism of American interference and the idea that Big Minh and the other generals were American puppets.

The point was rammed home by Ambassador Lodge, as I discovered when a friend in America sent me a copy of *The New York Times,* in which Lodge insisted during an interview that "We never participated in the planning. We never gave any advice. We had nothing whatever to do with it [the coup]. We were punctilious in drawing that line."

It was all nonsense, of course. The United States was deeply involved and the plot, it can be assumed, had the blessing of President Kennedy, who insisted that a plane be placed at Diem's disposal to fly him out of Vietnam. An extremist took the law into his own hands and Diem died, just as another extremist took the law into *his* hands less than three weeks later when President Kennedy was assassinated.

Since I had arrested the chief of the air force single-handedly and used the air force to swing the coup toward success, I can hardly be blamed if my thoughts turned to the possibility that I might succeed the man I had arrested. I had reckoned without Colonel Mai, the chief of staff, who had been at the gates.

It was Mai who had asked me to arrest his boss, Colonel Hien. While I was doing the dirty work, Mai, a shrewd operator, jumped into his car and made for the coup headquarters, where he explained how he had "organized" the downfall of his superior officer. He then blithely proposed that he should take over.

General Khiem, possibly without giving the matter much thought, agreed. I received a telegram promoting me to the rank of full colonel. (In those days we followed the American pattern of army ranks in the air force.) Mai became the boss of the air force.

I was disappointed, but then a curious thing happened. What I can only describe as spontaneous indignation spread throughout all ranks in the air force, particularly among those who had flown with me, trained with me, and were young and anxious to play a more active role in the war. I did not realize quite what was going on, though I did sense a strange undercurrent among my friends. The feeling was so powerful that it reached all the way back to the presidential palace, and Big Minh himself—a basic feeling that I should have been appointed chief of the air force since I had masterminded the air force role in the coup. I ignored the vague rumors I heard, but ten days after the coup I had to pilot Big Minh to a ceremony outside Saigon. As we landed he turned to me with a grin, and said, "Ky, I've decided to name you commander of the air force."

It is curious, the part destiny plays in shaping our lives. To me that promotion was the beginning of a new life. To Colonel Hien it was the end of his air force career, for Big Minh wisely decided to demobilize him.

However, Hien was a first-class pilot and within months I was able to use my influence to get him a job with Air Vietnam. Before long he was piloting a big jet, earning far more money than I could ever hope to earn as chief of the air force.

5

1964:

The year of the seven coups

For nearly two years after the death of Diem—until I became prime minister—South Vietnam was rent by political chaos. Nothing seemed to go right. Prime ministers came and went, and sometimes came back again. Coups were commonplace, though, fortunately, little blood was spilled. Exasperated Americans, anxious to promote a picture of stability, tried in vain to offer well-meaning advice. But two factors—one a broad political problem, the other a problem of human reaction in finer focus—thwarted all efforts.

The general problem was this: by insisting that the hated President Diem should remain in power for so long and then discarding him so abruptly, the Americans created a political vacuum which only the Communists were able to exploit. We were not capable of filling that vacuum because we did not know what to do. We had jumped from being a colony ruled by the French to being a country dependent on America, and the transition from independence French style to independence American style was so swift that we never had the opportunity to learn the art of governing ourselves unaided and uninfluenced. This was bad enough, but the malaise was compounded by another problem. Had the Americans arrived in our country with clear-cut ideas, we might have learned. However, they arrived full of good intentions but without any real understanding of the problems involved, without any real policy, and so took refuge in makeshift accommodations. And there is a world of difference between pursuing a policy and taking measures. We never learned how to pursue a policy, only the doubtful art of taking measures. Improvisation, usually in the form of a coup, was all we could think of in a country dominated by other races. If the first Americans had arrived and taught us the art of government, especially the art of compromise in governing, how different the end might have been. Instead they tried to run the Saigon government by Capitol Hill methods. They never understood that it is impossible to impose a Western mask on an Eastern face. The more one tries, the more one fails, as the defeat of both France and America in our country proves.

So we drifted, "taking measures." But in addition to our lack of knowledge and America's lack of policy, we faced the fine-focus problem: the reaction to the Diem coup among the average Vietnamese, who had hated Diem for years, and who hailed his downfall with the fervor of those taking part in a revolution—until the disillusion set in. Even though the end of the Diem regime became known as "the November Revolution," it never was a revolution. It was a coup, and that is vastly different.

A military coup is a carefully organized plot; a revolution is an uprising of the people, sometimes spontaneous, sometimes plotted, but always involving the people. When Big Minh took over from Diem it was a military and political power struggle in which the people were never consulted. Yet, wrongly, the people regarded it as a revolution, forgetting that, though the men who organized the coup against Diem might have been skilled at plotting the overthrow of a rival, it did not follow that they would be good enough to lead the country.

There was a second reason for the lack of stability. The Military Revolutionary Council—the supreme body responsible for electing government members—was not sufficiently united to select effective leaders and give them complete support. Members of the council had no common ideals and policies; they were opportunists rather than idealists. Their first loyalty was to their own careers rather than to their country. I did not realize this fully at the time, but I did later when I became prime minister and came to know them better. The Military Revolutionary Council members began squabbling among themselves almost immediately, and by mid-January those seeking preferment were planning another coup.

The man behind it was General Nguyen Khanh, a short, jaunty figure who sported a goatee and liked to wear his paratrooper's red beret. His favorite saying was "I'm a fighter," and he was. In his mid-thirties, he had fought as a guerrilla against the French. His mother kept a bar in Dalat, and his stepmother was a famous Vietnamese torch singer.

Khanh was an old friend and I liked him. I first heard about the projected coup early in January when Khanh mentioned casually—almost too casually—that he was unhappy about the way Big Minh was running the country. He said nothing about staging a coup, but he was testing my reactions, and basically I agreed with Khanh. I, too, was not happy with Big Minh. After all, like Khanh, I belonged to the younger generation, and though I had played my part in overthrowing Diem, we seemed to be no better off than we were. We saw the same old faces around the cabinet table. It was like shuffling the same old pack of cards. The Diem coup had taken place on November 1; by the end of January Khanh took over. It was not a coup in the dramatic sense of the word, for General Khanh and his followers simply confronted Big Minh and accused him and his followers in the Military Revolutionary Council of being neutralist. This was a time when anti-Communist feeling was welling up over the whole of South Vietnam, so neutralism was an emotive condemnation.

Big Minh and the leading members of the cabinet were deposed. I was not at the base on the night of the coup, but at seven o'clock the following morning one of my officers called me and said, "I think something happened; you had better go to the base." I raced back and it was lucky I did because within half an hour Khanh himself called me and said, "Ky, Big Minh and most of the members of his government have been kicked out. Are you with me or not?" I told him I was. From that moment Khanh was assured of victory, because he did not have to worry about the air force.

The year 1964 was like a crazy political seesaw, with seven changes of government. No sooner had Khanh overthrown Big

Minh than he re-appointed Big Minh chief of state (on American insistence) while Khanh himself became prime minister—with more power, of course. But by August Big Minh was out again and Khanh was chief of state. A month later Big Minh was back as chief of state and Khanh was premier once more.

During this time Khanh and I both came into disfavor with the Americans for urging them to step up the war. The Americans had contingency plans for doing just that, largely because they had no faith in the Khanh government and felt they must take on a larger role in the direction of the war.

But when Khanh had asked Secretary of Defense Robert McNamara earlier in the year to start attacking the North, McNamara stalled, saying that while he did not rule out the possibility, such action would have to be supplementary to, and not a substitute for, South Vietnamese action against the Communists in the South.

Then in July Khanh spoke at a rally in Saigon and announced a "March North" campaign, demanding that we carry the war north of the 17th parallel. On the same day I talked to some reporters on the need to bomb the Laotian trails used by the Viet Cong to infiltrate men and supplies into the South.

The Americans were furious with us—not because we were too daring but because they had made plans for both these operations. The Pentagon had drafted a scenario for graduated open war against the North, involving the bombing of specified targets, and had already begun deploying B-57s at Bien Hoa. After reconnaissance by U-2 planes, they had prepared a list of twenty-two targets inside Laos to be hit in an operation code-named "Barrel Roll."

They accused me of spilling the beans about Barrel Roll and never believed me when I swore ignorance of their plans. They accused Khanh of breaking faith with McNamara after being warned off a campaign against the North. Ambassador Maxwell Taylor feared that if no action followed the "March North" call, the South Vietnamese would become dissatisfied with the United States military. He was particularly fearful that one of my pilots might take off without authority and drop bombs on Hanoi, touching off an extension of hostilities.

But with the chaos prevailing in the South Vietnam government, I cannot believe that either Khanh or I caused any damage by our words.

In September Khanh was nearly kicked out again. In fact I saved him. It was Sunday, the 13th, a day I remember because it was the first time I took my future wife, Mai, out for the day. I drove her out of Saigon to visit the airfield at Bien Hoa, thirty-five miles to the north. On the way my aide commented on the number of troops on the move but, perhaps because of Mai's presence beside me, I paid no particular attention at the time.

However, by the time we got to Bien Hoa, the fact had registered. I called my headquarters in Saigon, asked for a helicopter to come to collect Mai and myself, and ordered fighter-bombers into the air to reconnoiter.

When the pilots contacted me by radio they told me: "Troops are entering Saigon. What are your orders?"

I told them to check whose troops they were and they reported back that they belonged to General Duong Van Duc, commander in chief in the Mekong River area.

I knew Duc, and I suddenly felt an uneasy sense of partial responsibility. Obviously Duc was trying to seize power, and a week earlier Duc and I had talked about Khanh, who was showing signs of developing a dictator complex, and I had said, "Something will have to be done about that man." Duc had taken my remark as implying more than I meant, and, without warning, he had committed a division of troops with tanks to a coup. By the time I landed the helicopter in Saigon, Duc controlled most of the city, including the army headquarters and the radio station.

I knew he would be hoping for my air support, but then I heard the voice of General Lam Van Phat on the radio. A friend of Duc's, he made several announcements I did not like. His announced aim was to restore the philosophy of Diem and he also hoped to draw on Diem's established reputation.

I had no faith in Phat. When I realized he was working with Duc, I called Duc and told him: "You have acted in a way I cannot support. Your wisest course is to return to camp."

Instead he sent his tanks to ring my air base. It was dark as they moved into position but flares lit the sky. I went to the perimeter, found the commander of the tank crews and warned him: "If you move one tank one foot more, I will have you bombed." The tanks did not move. The troops had no quarrel with the air force and did not really understand what was happening.

In the morning I called Duc again and told him: "It is time for you to give up. This is my ultimatum. If you do not withdraw, I shall bomb your army headquarters."

He gave up.

All this time Vietnam was not only fighting a war, but slowly preparing for the moment when the military would hand over power to the civilians. I was in favor of this move, provided the civilians were good enough. But the trouble was that all around us the decisions seemed to be taken by old men. When, as a first step toward eventual civilian rule, a nine-man High National Council (HNC) was formed in September 1964 to prepare a new constitution, the chairman, Dr. Phan Khac Suu, was in his nineties.

As the HNC started work, the Military Revolutionary Council agreed that General Khanh should step down as prime minister; he was replaced by a sixty-one-year-old schoolmaster, Tran Van Huong, former mayor of Saigon. All this was a temporary measure until the constitution was formed and elections could be held. Khanh remained head of the army.

Huong was a disaster. He had no drive, no foresight, and, worst of all, no guts when dealing with the thousands of rioters fighting in the Saigon streets against his weak and ineffectual government.

The idea behind the HNC was splendid—or would have been had we not been engaged in a life-and-death struggle against Communism. Within a few weeks it became obvious that the HNC had its head in the clouds. The council was so senile it was called the High National Museum in the bars of Saigon. But now I was able to do something about it at last, whereas before young men had had to sit back and watch the old men make a mess of things. The reason for the change was simple: ever since I had prevented the Phat coup against Khanh, I had become a sort of unofficial leader of a group of young officers who were not afraid to speak their minds. One newspaper writer christened us "The Young Turks." The name stuck.

We had no political ambitions. I was uninterested in politics. As chief of the air force, and a trained pilot, I just wanted to get a move on, go into the attack, kill Communists, save our country. That is what war is about. This was no time for doddering old civilians with one foot in the grave to direct the destiny of a country like ours. I believe, and believed then, in free elections, just as I believe in civilian rule, but this was war, and as Ambassador Lodge once remarked, "We had to win the war before we could indulge in the 'luxury' of politics."

I wanted to see a social revolution inside South Vietnam. There were still too many reminders of colonial days with too few ruling too many. We still had profiteers among the big businessmen and landowners. There was a great divide between the powerful minority and the powerless majority. Given a social revolution and equal opportunities for all to lead free and decent lives, I felt that the menace of Communism would evaporate.

My followers and myself were young, enthusiastic, and well trained; we had won quick promotion in the armed forces while the army itself was young. In fact most of us were founder members of the armed forces, for we had graduated straight from school to officers' training corps. We did not want to overthrow governments but to use our influence on those in office to bring about reforms speedily.

We were not only younger than the politicians around us, but we came from families more in touch with the people than the older rulers. Men like Diem had never been in touch with the people. Nor had the chairman of the HNC, Dr. Suu.

But the Young Turks felt for our country with our guts, not our heads. Our loyalties were single-minded, not torn by ties with the past. Old men like Suu *had* to be influenced by the past, by the French, even if subconsciously, whereas we despised the French for what they had done to our country.

We held no secret cabals to plot against leaders like Huong.

Our beliefs, our thirst for action, our demand for youth to have some say in our destiny, were spontaneous, perhaps because the Young Turks were also *active* Turks leading bombing raids or parachuting behind enemy lines.

All the same the time came when we had to act. And it was Khanh who persuaded us. Though he was out of office, Khanh was still popular. He was worried by the activities of the HNC, particularly of Big Minh, who was a power in the council, and some of his colleagues who were starting to foment unrest and divide army loyalties.

By now the Young Turks were meeting almost daily, usually half a dozen top officers, never more than ten. Sometimes we met at General Thi's paratroop headquarters, sometimes at the office of General Nguyen Huu Co, mostly at the air base where I lived. Khanh himself often came and joined in our discussions. At one such meeting at General Staff headquarters in mid-December 1964, Khanh said, "Some of the members of the High National Council are plotting for total power." We knew that Big Minh was not to be trusted, and one man—I think it was Thi—cried, "Who the hell do they think they are?" Someone else shouted, "Let's arrest them."

We held a vote by show of hands, and we decided there and then to arrest them. I remember it was around dusk and General Co (who later was part of my cabinet until I dismissed him for corruption) looked at his watch and cried, "It's getting late. It's time to round up the chickens and put them in the coop."

There were no problems. Khanh was head of the armed forces, I was in complete control of the air force. Others controlled the Special Forces, marines, paratroopers. I sent for junior officers, gave them details, and they sent the military police to arrest Big Minh and four others in their homes. The next day I flew them to Pleiku in the Highlands, where for some time they were kept under discreet house arrest.

We had all spent the night in billets at the General Staff headquarters, and I had hardly given the orders to fly the prisoners north before the telephone rang. The American embassy wished to speak to Khanh. We watched as Khanh listened attentively, occasionally saying a noncommittal "Yes" or "No," but when he finally put down the phone, he turned around and said, "Taylor wants to see us all at the American embassy right away. Well, I'm not going, I can tell you that. Which of you will represent me?" No one volunteered. Khanh turned to me and said, "Come on, Ky, you are the leader of the Young Turks, you had better go." Thieu and Thi agreed to accompany me. So did Admiral Chung Tan Cang.

We never really forgave Khanh for ducking the session at the embassy, for it was a very unpleasant hour!

General Maxwell Taylor, who was American ambassador to Saigon in 1964 and 1965, was a typical product of West Point, with an excellent war record, for he had not only commanded an airborne division which took part in the liberation of Europe, but had commanded the Eighth Army in Korea. Though he was scholarly and very much decorated he could never forget that he was no longer on parade as a general. His neat white civilian suit could not disguise his military attitude while he addressed us. Taylor was the sort of man who addressed people rather than talked to them.

We all trooped into his office overlooking the courtyard with its giant tamarind tree that one ambassador said signified America's strength in Vietnam. Taylor motioned us to seats and started abruptly, "Do all of you speak English?" We nodded, though, in fact, Thi's English was weak.

"Well," said Taylor, "I told you all clearly at General West-moreland's dinner that we Americans are tired of coups. Apparently I wasted my words."

His voice was at first difficult to follow, until I had adjusted to listening to a foreign tongue. Though he spoke fluent French he chose to speak in English, and for the moment I thought he was complaining that we had not liked Westmoreland's dinner. "But it was a wonderful dinner," I said cheerfully.

Taylor looked startled for a moment, then ignored my interruption. "I told you we were tired of coups," he repeated. "Apparently I wasted my words." Then, with a feeble attempt at heavy sarcasm, he added, "Maybe there is something wrong with my French because you evidently didn't understand. I thought I made it clear that all our military plans depend on

government stability. Now *you*"—he looked directly at me—
"have made a real mess. We cannot carry you forever if you do
things like this." Nobody had been able to get a word in, but
now he looked at us again and asked, "Who speaks for this
group? Do you have a spokesman?"

Knowing that I spoke the best English I replied, "I'm not the
spokesman for the group, but I do speak English. I will explain
why the armed forces took this action last night. We are aware
of our responsibilities, Mr. Ambassador, and we are aware of
the sacrifices of our people during the past twenty years. What
is more, we know you want stability. But you should know that
you cannot have stability until you have unity. And how can
you have unity when there are rumors of coups every day? We
know—and that is something you do *not* know, Mr. Ambassador
—that these rumors come from members of the High National
Council."

Slowly I explained to Taylor the signs we had seen over the
months, signs that indicated a split in the army which would
have been disastrous for Vietnam. I told him about a letter the
prime minister had received from a member of the HNC
warning him to beware of the military. Thieu interrupted to
say, "The HNC cannot be bosses because of the constitution.
Their members must prove that they want to fight." To which
I added, "It looks as though the HNC does not want unity. It
does not want to fight Communists."

Then I asked Taylor, "Why do you think we want to retire
generals like Big Minh? It's because they had their chance
and did badly."

The Young Turks, I said, had taken six hours to reach the
decision to arrest not only some members of the HNC, but also
bad student leaders, leaders of the Committee of National
Salvation, which was Communist-dominated.

"But," I added slowly, "we have no political ambitions. We
seek strong, unified, and stable armed forces to support the
struggle, and a stable government. Chief of State Suu agrees
with us. We did what we did for the good of our country. Now
I, personally, am ready to go back to my unit and fight."

"I respect the sincerity of you gentlemen," said Taylor, "but now I'd like to talk about the consequences of what you have done. First of all," and he spoke very slowly, looking at me, "you cannot go back to your unit, General Ky. You are now up to your neck in politics. This is a military coup that has destroyed the government-making process that, to the admiration of the world, was set up last fall through the statesmanlike acts of the armed forces."

Taylor asked whether any of us wished to enter the government and replace Chief of State Suu or Prime Minister Huong. When I replied in the negative, adding that people would say it was a military coup, Taylor retorted, "People will say it anyway." Would any of us wish to depose Huong? We chorused "No." Would we join him? Again we said "No." Our quarrel was not with Huong—though he was completely ineffectual—but against divisive influences in the armed forces. The army was all-important, and we wanted unity, not secret plotting for preferment.

Still talking to us as errant schoolboys who had been caught stealing apples from an orchard, Taylor added, "I don't know whether we will continue to support you after this. Why don't you tell your friends before you act? I regret the need for my blunt talk today but we have lots at stake. You people have broken a lot of dishes and now we have to see how we can straighten out this mess."

I nearly cried, "The dishes were dirty," but thought better of it. Thieu was fuming as we reached our automobiles, and wanted to call an immediate press conference in which he would tell the world how an American ambassador had treated top Vietnamese generals like stupid boys. "Don't do it, Thieu," I argued. "It won't get us anywhere; it won't do any good. Let's concentrate instead on the war."

For, all this time, there was a war to be fought, and despite Taylor's stupid remark about my being unable to return to my unit, I was on a bombing raid over the North within weeks of our painful interview, when I led a flight of South Vietnamese planes in the operation "Flaming Dart I." It was the first reprisal strike on North Vietnam ordered by President Johnson, and took place in February 1965.

The Americans had been considering reprisals from the air for some time, mainly because the war was slowing down due to the political turmoil in Saigon. When the Viet Cong planted a bomb in the Brinks, an officers' billet in Saigon, killing two Americans and wounding fifty-eight, the United States Joint Chiefs of Staff pressed for immediate retaliation, but the president had declined to permit it.

But when the Communists attacked the military advisers' compound at Pleiku in the Central Highlands, and Camp Holloway, a United States helicopter base nearby, killing nine Americans and wounding seventy-six, the president decreed that there should be "an appropriate and fitting response." Both American and South Vietnamese planes were to administer the salutary lesson and the chosen target was Donghoi, a training establishment for guerrillas north of the 17th parallel.

I led the South Vietnamese flight into the air on a Sunday afternoon, little more than twelve hours after the Pleiku incident, but when we broke through the monsoon clouds over Donghoi I found the American aircraft, which had flown from the Seventh Fleet carriers *Coral Sea* and *Hancock*, already in action.

There were forty-nine of them—U.S. Navy A4 Skyhawk and F8 Crusader jets—pounding the Communists. To avoid collision I had to lead my flight away, and, since there seemed little point in punishing the target further, I found another target in the Vinhlinh area and we bombed that. Later we learned that this target was the headquarters of an antiaircraft regiment, and their return fire was ferocious. Every one of the twenty-four planes I was leading was hit. My own plane was struck by four bullets, one of which grazed my body as I lifted my arm in reflex to protect my face. I found that bullet and saved it for my wife. Two of my pilots were forced to bail out into the sea. All of the Vietnamese pilots in this raid were volunteers. The difficulties of this raid did not prevent the pilots from continuing to volunteer. In fact, it was many times the case that when we drew lots for the right to fly, those who lost would bribe the winners to take their place for the right to join in.

Of course, this had not been assigned by Washington and my action caused some friction between Washington and Saigon when Admiral U. S. Grant Sharp, commander of United States forces in the Pacific, reported it to the Joint Chiefs of Staff. I lost no sleep over this because I knew I had made the sensible decision at the time.

In any event, the reprisal strike was not the one-shot, tit-for-tat mission that was intended, because the Communists attacked another American barracks—at Qui Nhon—and Johnson ordered a second reprisal strike, "Flaming Dart II." And this led straight on to "Operation Rolling Thunder," the American campaign of sustained air warfare.

Rolling Thunder was scheduled originally to start on February 20, 1965, but was postponed because of another attempted coup by General Phat—and deep trouble for General Khanh.

6

YOUNG TURKS:

The road to power

By early 1965 it was evident that Prime Minister Huong was leading Vietnam to disaster, and at the end of January the Armed Forces Council (which had replaced the Military Revolutionary Council), which was much more united since Big Minh left, decided that Huong must go. There was no drama. The decision was conveyed to Huong, he accepted it gracefully (and probably thankfully!), and General Khanh assumed power.

Unfortunately he was changing. If it is true that power corrupts, it is also true that power deludes. We had all seen how Diem lived in a world of illusions. Now there were immediate signs that Khanh was becoming more dictatorial. He was not abusing his powers as Diem had done. He was doing nothing wrong. But—just as bad—he was doing nothing right.

The Young Turks were by now the power behind the throne, and it soon became necessary to warn Khanh that he was losing the goodwill of the people and the respect of the fighting forces.

Shortly after my bombing mission, I went to see Khanh in the prime minister's office. I had ready access to Khanh, for not only were we old friends—there was never any animosity between us—but he also realized he needed the support of the Young Turks. It was this that made me warn him. We were alone.

I knew that Khanh was a highly astute politician, but sometimes one can be too clever, and I felt this was the case now. Bitterness was erupting between Catholics and Buddhists, between rival political factions, and Khanh seemed to stoke the fires of discontent deliberately. "That's fine for colonialists," I said, "they like to divide and rule, but you're not a colonialist, you are prime minister of Vietnam, and you must do everything to unite our country. You must listen to me, General," I added. "We all want to support you, but if you want to keep that support, please don't try and play politics."

I went a step further. "You've got to be tougher," I said, "and take strong measures to stop demonstrations that are against the national interest." I was thinking of one instance when Khanh sent troops to quell a disturbance, but had forbidden them to carry loaded rifles. What good is an unarmed soldier against an unruly mob? "If you can't get tougher," I ended up, "you should resign. Otherwise the country will blame you— and your children will be ashamed of you."

As I reached the door, Khanh smiled and said, "I know what you mean, Ky—but remember, you are young and impetuous. . . ."

I realized he would do nothing. "But I'm only telling you what we feel—what the country feels," I said. "We *are* young, but the Young Turks are the pulse of the nation."

Looking back now, I can see that Khanh never really believed that we young people were determined enough to force our demands on any government. So nothing really changed.

Soon after this some of us decided that Khanh must go. I myself made the decision to organize a coup when I heard that Khanh was visiting the Mekong Delta area to meet troops of the Fourth Corps, commanded by Thieu, one of us. Khanh planned to stay the night at 9th Division headquarters at Can Tho, and I telephoned Thieu, saying, "We've got to do something. The country is heading for stalemate. Now we've got Khanh out of the capital, let's strike. I'll fly down in a separate plane when he leaves Saigon, and we'll make plans to arrest him."

After talking plans over with Thieu, I told him, "I'll fly back to Saigon now and tell the others of our plan. Don't do anything until I've got their okay. Then I'll phone you."

To my astonishment the "okay" was never given. Several

members of the Young Turks felt we were acting too hastily, that the timing was not right. So the coup was canceled.

Within days, however, Khanh's fate was sealed by General Phat, who attempted another coup on February 18. Even though it was unsuccessful, Khanh was shrewd enough to see the writing on the wall.

At 11:30 on the morning of February 19, 1965, I was at home playing mah jongg with half a dozen pilots when Khanh telephoned me. "I think something has happened," he said. "There are a lot of tanks on the move."

I told my pilots, "Go back to your squadrons, take off and have a look around." But they had hardly left the room before they were back again. "We can't get to the hangars. There are tanks everywhere," they reported.

I leapt into a jeep and set off alone. At the gate I met Khanh in his Mercedes, flying his official flag. There was no way to drive past the tanks converging on the air base, so I told him to get out and walk past them. No one stopped him as he slowly walked toward me.

"Phat is practically in control of Saigon," he said. "Can you get me out of here?"

"I don't think I can," I replied. "My pilots couldn't take off. Where do you want to go?"

"The Mekong," he said—it seemed to me almost at random, though I remembered that his mother lived at Dalat. "Anywhere, but let's get out of here."

"Well, if we do go, we'd better be quick," I retorted.

I knew a back way to a hangar where an emergency plane was always kept ready for takeoff. We raced around there in my jeep, keeping out of sight of Phat's troops, who did not seem to be coming any farther into the base.

I pushed Khanh into a passenger seat, revved up the engine, and then took the plane to the runway. We were just in time, for as I turned toward the end of the runway, I saw twenty tanks trundling toward us from the far end. I couldn't go back, so I gave the old DC3 full power and raced down the runway, almost skimming the tanks with my wheels as we took off.

Once airborne Khanh seemed to relax. "I don't know what

to do," he said, "but I want you to take me to Dalat. Then I give you a free hand to act as you think best." He repeated, "You have my full authority to handle the problem."

"Right," I said, "I'll keep you informed." I landed near Dalat, dropped Khanh, then set off south again. I could not land at Saigon, for Phat's troops ringed the base, so I made for Bien Hoa, some twenty miles to the north. It was still in government hands. As soon as I landed I took over the office of the commander—temporarily, of course. The first thing I did was to summon a cabinet meeting to be held in Bien Hoa. I wonder, thinking back, how I dared to. After all, I had no written authority from Khanh, only his word. On the other hand, everybody knew that Phat was in virtual control of Saigon. Members of the cabinet and members of the Armed Forces Council started arriving, mostly by road. General Thi flew in from Danang. When the forty or so men were assembled, I told what had happened. Everyone was unhappy at the turn of events, and everyone was apprehensive about the future under Khanh.

"There is one thing," I insisted. "I don't think we can make a momentous decision of this nature unless Khanh is present. It's only fair. I think he ought to be able to state his point of view."

It was an attitude to politics and power that I have always believed in, and Khanh was very touched. I sent a plane to pick him up and he arrived within a couple of hours. But I could see that he obviously felt the tension in the room as he faced his colleagues. Some clamored for his resignation, and others cried for him to stay. He passed a hand across his eyes, and said simply, "I would like to go back to Dalat. It's up to Ky, and all of you, to decide what's going to be done—whether you support Phat or me—or, for that matter, anyone else."

Abruptly he walked out of the room. The plane that had flown him up was waiting, and as I walked alone with Khanh across the runway, I knew he was wondering whether that "anyone else" might be myself, that I might be plotting secretly to seize power, though if he nursed any such suspicions they were unfounded. As we shook hands before he climbed in, he said, "Well, Ky, if you want to do something, I can't stop you. But don't be rash, and don't forget our friendship, all the good times we have had together."

When I returned to the conference room the atmosphere was totally different, now that the restraining and embarrassing presence of poor Khanh was no longer there. Everyone demanded change, but I demanded something else: *legal* change. "We've had too many old-fashioned military takeovers," I said. "If we make any changes now, they must be made legally. The first thing we have to do is get back to Saigon, then send for Dr. Suu of the High National Council to draw up a decree authorizing any changes."

But before we could return to Saigon, we had to get rid of Phat. I decided to use the same threat of air power that had served me well in the past, and I was about to try and make contact with Phat when, without warning, General Robert Rowland, American adviser to the Vietnam air force, telephoned me at 3 P.M. and said: "My government wants to know whether you are with the rebels." I told him I was not and said, "You had better tell those people to get out of my headquarters in Saigon. Tell them that I give them four hours; that is, until 7 P.M. If they don't go, I shall bomb the Saigon area."

It very nearly came to that. At 6:30 Rowland called me again. "Now, Ky, don't do it. Apart from anything else, I'm at headquarters, and if you bomb it, you'll bomb me too."

I told him I had no alternative.

At five minutes to seven Rowland rang again. "Suppose I bring Phat and Colonel Thao, who is with him, to see you. Will you guarantee safe conduct?"

Colonel Pham Ngoc Thao, a Catholic, had once been a Vietminh officer. I had not seen him since before the Diem coup in 1963 but I knew that he had been involved with Duc and Phat in the previous abortive coup. He was something of a mystery man, pushing dissident generals from behind.

I agreed and canceled my orders to bomb headquarters.

Colonel Freund of the U.S. Army flew with Phat and Thao to

Bien Hoa. The coup ended the following morning when I sent observation planes ahead of a force of paratroopers and tanks, dropping messages to Phat's troops saying: "Do not resist or Ky will bomb you." The opposition crumbled.

Thao and Phat fled, hiding for two years in Catholic villages. Thao met a grisly end. When police discovered where he was hiding they persuaded Thao's bodyguard, a man actually paid by the police to report on Thao, to meet him at a rendezvous, where the man Thao had trusted shot him in the neck and left him for dead. But when the police arrived, Thao had vanished. He had only been wounded. However, police found him twenty-four hours later and threw him in jail, where he was shot on orders from General Thieu. It was, I believe, Thieu who had earlier arranged for the bodyguard to shoot him. When I became prime minister, I granted amnesty, bringing Phat out of hiding. During the last few weeks before the fall of Saigon he came often to my house to offer his cooperation in helping to overthrow Thieu. To my knowledge, Phat is still in Saigon.

The day after the coup fizzled out we decided what should be done with Khanh. None of the Young Turks wished him any harm; we just wanted him out of the way, and I found the perfect solution. We appointed him roving ambassador. He was speeded on his way by a dignified ceremonial farewell at the airport. I personally went aboard the plane to say good-bye and wish him well.

For a few weeks all was quiet. The ancient Suu remained as chief of state and we elected as temporary premier a civilian, Phan Huy Quat. There were no problems for several months, though there were rumors that the two men were finding it difficult to get on with each other.

Finally Quat summoned all ministers and members of the Armed Forces Council to a hastily convened cabinet meeting at the premier's office at 8 P.M. on June 12. I remember walking in to the office and, as we waited, helping myself to food from a cold buffet laid out on a long trestle table in a corner of the room. There were beer and soft drinks on another table.

To some it seemed that the differences between the two men hinged on the interpretation of law. They could never agree. "I can't really go on," wailed Quat, "because the chief of state tries to prevent me from doing anything."

My own feeling is that they just happened to dislike each other bitterly, and were always trying to score off each other instead of working hand in hand.

Suu was present—in body if not in spirit, for one could never pin the old man down; he drooled on, making wandering speeches about the rule of law and manners in politics. Finally Quat banged on his desk and, without any preamble, announced brusquely, "I resign. And since it was the Armed Forces Council that named me premier, I hand back that power to the council."

We had half expected it. Prime ministers do not telephone in the night to arrange cabinet meetings unless there is an emergency. But now we ran into a time-consuming problem, in the shape of that old dotard, Suu. For hours we could get no action out of him. My view was that if power were handed back to the military, it should be authorized and legalized so that General Thieu, who I imagined would be premier, would be elected on firm ground. Suu was the chairman of the HNC, and we needed his signature to the decree. But he kept talking about "differences I can resolve." He was in the clouds. Finally, about 12:30 A.M., I whispered to two men next to me, "Go out into the next room and write out the declaration announcing Quat's desire to hand over power to the Armed Forces Council. Bring it to me. Try and find a tape recorder and bring that along too."

The two men drafted out a decree as Suu rambled on, demanding almost plaintively, "Why is my dear friend Quat deserting me?" While we waited, we munched sandwiches, until finally the two officers returned with the decree and the tape machine. I placed the declaration in front of Suu, next to the tape recorder, and pleaded, "Please, Mr. Chief of State, would you read this message. We don't have any more time to discuss things."

Without demur, indeed with a look of relief, Suu read the message aloud, apparently approvingly. One of us grabbed it, and then, dead tired, we all made for our homes.

The question of electing a new prime minister could wait until the morrow.

The next morning all the fifty high-ranking members of the Armed Forces Council—which, of course, included all the Young Turks—and the cabinet assembled to elect a new prime minister. We decided to hold the meeting in the marine headquarters, which contained a large, formal meeting room for staff conferences, with rows of tip-up chairs, rather like cinema seats, and in place of a stage a large oval table where Major General Thieu, as the senior official, presided at the meeting, seated in the center, with the heads of the commands grouped around him. None of us could possibly have imagined that we would stay two days and a night there before a new leader of Vietnam was nominated.

After Thieu had explained the purpose of the meeting, I stood up, as the acknowledged leader of the Young Turks, and said, "I propose General Thieu should be elected." After all Thieu was senior officer, and I imagined he would have no difficulty in obtaining the required number of votes.

To my astonishment Thieu thanked me, but flatly refused to stand for election.

At this, of course—human nature being what it is—there were cries of "We need you" and "Don't disappoint us." No doubt many of them came from the fence-sitters who follow the wind, but who had not thought fit to suggest Thieu in the first place. For an hour or more we tried to persuade Thieu to stand. We all felt (at that time) that he would be a good leader for the country, but he was adamant. He did not want the responsibility, he said. It was a remark I would never forget in the years to come.

We broke off for a lunch of sandwiches, washed down with beer or American soft drinks, and when we reassembled I proposed General Co. He refused too, but his refusal led to hours more of debate and argument. Finally, exhausted, we decided to close the meeting about 10 P.M. and reconvene the following morning. Beds were provided and we all had supper in the Officers' Mess.

The next morning I had a sudden brainwave.

"I propose General Thi," I said.

Brigadier General Nguyen Chan Thi, commander of First Corps, had a reputation as a courageous paratrooper—an active one who always jumped with his men—and he always liked the limelight. I knew from the kinds of remarks he made that he fancied himself as a bit of a political animal, and I said so now. "After all," I added, "you would be perfect. You are more politically inclined than most generals, and you enjoy the limelight."

But Thi not only refused once, he cried, "No, no, no, never."

Of course everyone who refused the job knew perfectly well that we were going through an extremely difficult phase in which the chances of failing loomed larger than any slim hopes of success. And the army, being the army, breeds a kind of man who instinctively hates the idea of being associated with an unsuccessful mission. I do not mean this in a disparaging way; it is merely an inbred army trait: you don't get promotion unless you succeed.

To me those two days of "No, no, no" are still unbelievable, though it is true that in those difficult years the international press had created something of a negative public opinion about the office. Any man who accepted the mantle of premiership was immediately exposing himself to a possible hammering by public opinion, to opposition from every possible party. Once you became prime minister of Vietnam in those chaotic days you not only ran the risk of being ignominiously overthrown, but the danger of assassination. Perhaps that thought lurked in more minds than one during those two incredible days.

I can say honestly that it never entered my mind that I was a suitable candidate for election. We needed a military government to follow Quat and Suu, but while the army and navy totaled hundreds of thousands of men, the air force in those days was only about 30,000 strong. The fledglings might have learned to fly, but they were puny compared to the big boys of the army.

Then, after we had broken for yet another coffee break,

the bombshell broke. In a corner I saw Thieu, Co, and Thi talking earnestly, and then Thieu walked toward me in the lobby and said bluntly, "Ky, why don't *you* accept the role of prime minister? No one else wants the job, no one else dares to take it."

"I think Thieu should be our next prime minister," I insisted, "but if he won't do it, I know one thing. If this ridiculous meeting lasts only a few more hours, power will pass *away* from the armed forces."

"We must get it right," said Thieu.

"Imagine if you were a civilian cabinet minister," I said. "What on earth would you think of an army that can't decide who shall be its political boss? I can imagine the civilians thinking, 'What sort of an army is that to win the war for us?' We've been offered the chance of power. The civilians have made a mess of it. So, until the time comes for a civilian government to return, we need a strong man—a military man."

"You stand, *please*," Thieu pleaded.

Again I hesitated. I really knew nothing about politics, only what I believed in for my country.

Finally I said, "One way or another, the military *must* form a government as soon as possible. If none of the others dares to accept the responsibility, and if you all really have enough confidence in me, then I am ready to accept it as I've always accepted any job—even the hardest—that the armed forces assigned to me."

We went back into the meeting. Thieu proposed me for prime minister and the entire meeting erupted into cheers. I got what Westerners call a standing ovation.

I still wanted to make doubly certain that no one else wanted the job, and stood up once more before the assembled officers, asking them, "If anyone would like to step out and take my place, please do so!" There was a chorus of "No."

At this stage I had, of course, made no plans. A strong believer in destiny, I had never imagined this day coming to pass, so I had none of the long-range schemes that plotters usually have stored away.

All I could say in my acceptance speech was that I was

proud of the great honor offered to me as a member of the Armed Forces Council rather than as a politician. I was not, I told the audience, a member of any political party. The only thing I *did* know was that I did not want total power for myself, but hoped to be able to form quickly a team that would work with me, so that everyone in the government would feel involved in all the decisions we made. And then I added one condition. "I will have to ask my wife for her authorization."

My wife's first reaction was: "No way." A young married couple, we did not like politics, we had no desire to get mixed up with political intrigues. However, as I explained the facts to her, she understood and went along with my decision. The next day, I returned to the armed forces conference and confirmed my acceptance.

7

PRIME MINISTER:

My three days with Johnson

During the hectic days of the Young Turks, I had not only been involved in coups and aerial combat, I had fallen in love. My first marriage, to a Frenchwoman, by whom I had five children, had ended in separation and then divorce, after which, in the words of one newspaperman, I enjoyed "two highly eventful years as a lady killer."

While it is not for me to say how exaggerated that report was, I did have a lot of fun, for all of us in those days existed on a razor's edge, and life had to be lived for the moment. But in 1964, I flew as a passenger on Air Vietnam to Bangkok on an official visit. The twenty-year-old air hostess was the most classically beautiful girl I had ever seen.

Her name was Dang Tuyet Mai, and I persuaded her to dine with me that evening. The following morning, knowing that her return flight was leaving early, I felt I must say good-bye. But Vietnamese men do not just barge into ladies' bedrooms at 6 A.M. However, I found a way. I was already dressed in the starched white uniform of an air marshal, in readiness for an official parade, so I waylaid the waiter bringing her breakfast, slipped him a few *bhats*, and knocked politely on Mai's door. She was looking out of a window and hardly gave me a glance as she ordered me to put the tray down. Later she told me she was trying to catch a glimpse of me on my way to the parade!

Our courtship was brief. Mai's parents were at first opposed to her marrying a man who, they said, had an unsavory reputation with the ladies. Nor did they approve of the fact that though I might have been commander of the air force, I was still penniless. Those "two eventful years" had not been cheap. My attempts to ingratiate myself with Mai's parents were not helped when, after making a date with Mai and then being delayed on a secret mission, I tried to prove that I really had been flying by hovering over her parents' house in my helicopter at 4 A.M.

When we decided to get married, I bought a ring for the equivalent of twelve dollars, and Huong, then prime minister, gave us as a wedding present the princely sum of 200,000 piastres, which came in very handy for our wedding reception at the Hotel Caravelle where "everyone" was invited—not only Khanh and Huong, but the diplomatic corps and all my chums in the air force.

Khanh gave me a splendid present—his secondhand 1960 Ford Falcon, which he no longer needed because he had an official automobile. It was the first car I ever owned; until that moment, I had always driven a free jeep, and I treasured that car until the fall of Saigon.

We started our married life in my house on the air base, which was not really a house at all, but had originally been the base commander's office, to which I had added a few rooms for the children and myself. It was all I needed and I loved it so much that I had been dreading the moment when my bride would announce that we must move into a proper house. Not a bit of it. Mai loved the place, with its huge lounge and deep, comfortable armchairs. She called in the builders and decorators and set about transforming my bachelor quarters into married quarters. When I became prime minister, we decided to continue living on the base, although the security people insisted on building a wall around our garden and posted guards twenty-four hours a day. Since passes were also needed to enter the main gates, we felt quite safe.

Instead of moving to the prime minister's official residence, a three-story house about a mile from the presidential palace, I used it only as my office, though it did have kitchens and a staff and bedrooms so that I could entertain and sleep there when pressure of business kept me late—as it often did in those hectic days. I worked in my office, a large room with a handsome desk, comfortable armchairs for visitors, a conference table, and even a refrigerator. Large signed photographs of world leaders adorned the walls.

Kitchens, bedrooms, the refrigerator were all *necessary* to make life easier for a man in my position. It had to be so. I had to be able to lay on a supper for a dozen people at a moment's notice if discussions dragged on. No prime minister should have to worry about niggling problems.

With luxuries, however, it is very different. Power seems to breed in men a fascination for extravagant but unimportant items, and the fact that they are free gives them an added allure. On my very first day as prime minister, one of my battery of ten secretaries came to ask me what kind of official automobile I would like. "The Mercedes is very much in favor at the moment," he added.

"But I've got a car," I exclaimed.

"For your private use, I understand, Sir, but for official functions..."

"I'll stick to my Falcon for all occasions," I insisted, and I did throughout my term, while all my colleagues were pulling strings to try to acquire new and shiny automobiles slightly larger, if possible, than their rivals'. I was happy with my car, but I made no attempt to stop the others from getting cars for the job. I was too busy to try to buck the system.

It was hard sometimes to believe that I was prime minister. A week after I took office, my wife gave birth to our daughter, Duyen. I took time off to visit them both in the hospital, and during one such visit, a nurse asked me for information for the necessary forms. She came to one question and asked me, "Your profession, Sir?"

I must have hesitated, for she added with a smile, "Of course, Sir, prime minister."

"Oh no," I replied, "prime minister is not a profession; and being prime minister is certainly not my profession. My profession is pilot."

My first task was to form a government—a formidable task for one who had never been involved in any political activity —and did not belong to any party. Indeed, I knew hardly any politicians, and yet it was inconceivable to select only military officers for government posts. I enrolled the help of many civilians who joined me, perhaps because they believed I was sincere. My government was composed of old and young, Buddhists as well as Catholics, Northerners as well as Southerners. It was a government that successfully gathered together the most representative elements of Vietnam's social spectrum. Anyone who dared to call it a military government was talking nonsense. Only myself, as prime minister, the secretary of defense, and the home minister were military men. The rest of the cabinet—ministers of education, health, public affairs, and so on—were civilians, many with sympathies for the Buddhists. They even included a remarkable young Southerner, Au Truong Thanh, as minister of economics—remarkable because Thanh had a left-wing reputation and was even suspected of pro-Communist tendencies. But I asked him to participate in my government because I had faith in his abilities.

I made it a point never to make any critical decisions on my own. The policies of my new government were the results of the teamwork from all members of the cabinet. To say that mine was a military, dictatorial government is a downright lie, as all the witnesses who are still alive will verify.

My policies were very simple, in direct contrast to previous governments, when each new leader proposed lengthy and impossible programs that could never be fulfilled. When I presented my cabinet, I proposed sixteen basic points to be fulfilled by my government, a transitional government. First of all, re-establish stability, which had gradually disappeared since the end of Diem's regime. Secondly, build a solid foundation for future governments by establishing a true democratic system in South Vietnam. I remember the first time I met Henry Cabot Lodge, who had replaced Taylor, and Lodge asked me about my policies. I replied with two words: "Social justice." (At the same reception, Lodge introduced me to Edward Lansdale, who had arrived in Vietnam with the reputation of being a kingmaker following his activities in the Philippines. I told him: "Now that you are here, you will have no problems, because I have no intention of becoming a king."

When my government started to function, I confess I was a little bit lost at first. I had to spend some time simply learning about my role and my duty. And yet, there were no coups against me, no vociferous opposition. Could it be that the amateur was succeeding where the professionals had failed? It seemed so, for after I had been prime minister for a month, Thieu, the chief of state, said to me, "Let's have a celebration."

I asked why. "You've lasted a month," he cried. We had, indeed. And month after month we colleagues in the cabinet met every month to celebrate.

For they *were* colleagues—and this, if I am not being immodest, was a transformation in politics that I can claim to have brought to South Vietnam. Gone were the days of political chaos brought about by power plays and by disputes between different political factions. Right from the start I realized that concentration of power in one man inevitably leads to danger. I made sure it would not happen—not only to myself, but to any member of my cabinet who showed signs of power lust.

I wanted *collaboration* and I got it by setting up a ruling committee called the Committee of National Leadership, composed of powerful figures within the military, a dozen able civilians, and spokesmen for each political party. At the heart of the committee was the Executive Council—the government, with me as chairman. With the participation of civilian elements, the presence of political groups such as the Buddhists and Catholics, the Southerners and Northerners, and the people of the Midlands, there seemed to be no reason why I should not bring back stability to South Vietnam for the first time in many years.

Together, we achieved many successes. We instituted a large-scale program of wealth distribution to help the poor, shelter for the dispossessed, transport and equipment for workers, and augmentation of the rice ration and wages. No wonder that soon we earned the name "government of the poor." I can proudly say that the majority was satisfied: the military was satisfied with the government; the mass of the poor people, benefiting from a pragmatic approach to social programs, was also satisfied.

Gradually the press stopped referring to me as "the acting premier" or "prime minister in the provisional government." I became simply "the prime minister."

I had to be tough, but then I *could* be tough, for I was in a unique position since I had become premier only because no one else had the guts to take on the job. Anyone who is not a professional politician finds it much easier to say what he likes, speak his thoughts, be frank with everyone. There is no need to be devious. Politicians are different and it has always seemed to me that the more experienced a politician is, the more devious he tends to become. President Nixon was a supreme example of this.

Of course I had to watch my step. Since at heart I hated politics and had no experience, I tended at the beginning to speak too openly. Almost as soon as I became premier I made a speech in which I said, "The time has come for youth to guide the destiny of our nation. This is youth's opportunity; everyone over fifty is finished." This sweeping generalization offended everyone over fifty, including my uncle and my father's friends. I was not very popular at home for a time.

I was also embarrassed by a report that I had said we needed a Hitler in Vietnam. The British ambassador in Saigon came to see me and told me that left-wing members of Parliament in Britain were blocking efforts to provide aid for Vietnam because they said I was an admirer of Hitler.

"Look, Mr. Ambassador," I told him, "I never said I admired Hitler. All I can remember about the incident is that when I was in command of the air force I was having a chat with several American reporters and told them how much we needed strong leadership in South Vietnam. I cited the way in which a weak Germany had been turned into a great power by Hitler. I could just as easily have cited Ho Chi Minh, and that would have been equally unpopular. I abhorred the way Hitler used his power and I never presented him as my hero."

It did not take long to learn to present my thoughts more tactfully. Despite my lack of experience, I survived, and what is more, I helped write the constitution of Vietnam and I held the first free elections. None of the professional politicians could have done that, or would have ever dared to do it, because they were too experienced and consequently afraid of criticism. My lack of political knowledge helped me, for the people of Vietnam knew that even when I made mistakes they were honest mistakes. I was doing my best; I was not corrupt and I wanted only to help my country.

I summed up my feelings in one speech, "My aim is to be a strong leader of all the people of Vietnam—someone the people in the villages can trust, someone who can control the towns."

I put first things first: full bellies and a victory march had to come before American dreams of free elections. As I told the Americans, "Each time you go into the fields and say 'elections' the poor reply with one word, 'Food.'"

These and other beliefs caused the Americans to eye me at first with suspicion. I knew perfectly well that they thought of me, at first, as a "lightweight," with no knowledge of the political arena. Those Americans who actively disliked me did so only because I spoke the truth. I was not afraid even then to say what I reiterate now: American troops might be the world's upholders of democracy and freedom, but that was not the only reason they were in Vietnam. They were there to safeguard America's interests as well.

At first Thieu and I got on fairly well, but there was one curious difficulty between us. As chief of state he did not have any real power. I had to make the decisions and this made him jealous. I could have understood this better if Thieu had not declined the premiership before me because he was afraid of the responsibility. He wanted power and glory but he did not want to have to do the dirty work. That was the kind of man he was.

And there was dirty work to be done. I had to be tough, and I had to start with my cabinet colleagues. There has always been a tendency in Vietnamese politics for politicians to act on their own and, during my first week in office, a deputy from the North who had a grudge against a rival from the South used his power in a way I did not like. The other complained.

I waited until the cabinet met and then I told them both, "I am prime minister and if you want something changed, come and see me." Then, turning to the man from the North, I said, "If you feel that you can take the law into your own hands you had better resign right now." He did have the courage to stand up and offer his resignation immediately.

I stood for no nonsense from the cabinet. "We have to be a team," I said. "We must have one common, united policy. If you don't agree with me you can walk out. We are fighting a war and even if you all walk out I shall not change my attitude." One or two looked startled. "Perhaps you think that if all the prominent politicians refuse to work with me I might have difficulty in forming a cabinet," I added. "Not at all. I could form a cabinet in twenty-four hours. I would go to army headquarters and pick twenty-four good NCOs—I wouldn't even need officers."

They knew I was prepared to carry out my threat. I was determined that the government—military and civilians—should work as a team. For that, one had to demand absolute loyalty. I was completely ruthless, even when friends were involved.

I had become prime minister at a turning point in America's involvement in the war. On April 2, 1965—six weeks before I took office—President Johnson had made the decision that American ground troops should go over to offensive action.

I did not know this at the time, of course, but then nobody outside the presidential circle knew it; this decisive step was blanketed in secrecy. Johnson took it because it was apparent that the month-old bombing offensive could not alone stave off the collapse of South Vietnam with its ever-changing governments. Johnson did not dare to increase the bombing and risk Chinese intervention, so he ruled that the U.S. Marines should go on the offensive, and sanctioned the addition of another 18,000 to 20,000 men to reinforce the 57,000 Americans in Vietnam at the time. These comprised seven marine and four army battalions. General Westmoreland also had an Australian battalion under his command.

The decision was taken none too soon, for by June the Communist summer offensive was in full flow and Westmoreland realized he needed even more forces, as he told Washington in June. "The Viet Cong are capable of mounting regimental-size operations in all four South Vietnam corps areas," he said. "Desertion rates in the Vietnamese army are inordinately high. Battle losses have been higher than expected. I see no course of action open to us except to reinforce our efforts with additional United States or third country forces as rapidly as is practicable during the critical weeks ahead." He asked for a total force of forty-four battalions, a staggering increase of thirty-three.

It was at this point that the president's decision on the use of ground forces became public knowledge, together with the news that the U.S. Marines had sustained two hundred casualties. The White House issued a bland statement: "There has been no change in the mission of United States ground combat units in Vietnam in recent days or weeks. The president has issued no order of any kind in this regard to General Westmoreland recently or at any other time. The primary mission of these troops is to secure and safeguard important military installations like the air base at Danang. They have the associated mission of patrolling and securing actions in and near the areas thus safeguarded.

"If help is requested by the appropriate Vietnamese commander, General Westmoreland also has authority within the assigned mission to employ those troops in support of Vietnamese forces faced with aggressive attack when other effective reserves are not available and when, in his judgment, the general military situation urgently requires it."

This statement widened the credibility gap in the United States, but the gap became a chasm when America's 173rd Airborne Brigade went into action with the Australian battalion and South Vietnamese forces north of Saigon on June 27. For this three-day operation, the first of its kind the Americans had undertaken, was no "securing action"; it was what General Westmoreland called a "search and destroy" operation into Viet Cong areas. Westmoreland told me that his search and destroy tactics could defeat the enemy by the end of 1967.

Within a month of my taking office, Defense Secretary Mc-Namara came to Saigon to assess Westmoreland's forty-four-battalion request. He approved it. So did the United States Joint Chiefs of Staff—and by the end of the year there were 184,314 American troops in Vietnam and the number was rising, even though the White House still insisted there had been no change of policy on the use of American troops.

Meanwhile I was establishing my authority as prime minister. McNamara visited me before the end of 1965 and reported to the president, "The Ky government of generals is surviving, but not acquiring wide support or generating actions. Pacification is thoroughly stalled, with no guarantee that security anywhere is permanent, and no indications that able and willing leadership will emerge in the absence of that permanent security. Prime Minister Ky estimates that his government controls only 25 percent of the population today and reports that his pacification chief hopes to increase that to 50 percent two years from now."

Since my government had been in power less than five months and had to restore order from chaos, I felt the report was somewhat grudging, but McNamara went on to recommend providing still more troops for Westmoreland. It was not until the following year that he became disillusioned and joined the "doves."

After six months in office I derived new strength and authority from a meeting in Honolulu with President Johnson. The president was having difficulties with the Senate Foreign Relations Committee, which was conducting an inquiry into America's commitment in Vietnam. Senator William Fulbright, in particular, had questioned Johnson's right to send United States troops into battle.

At two days' notice Johnson called a conference that started on February 6, 1966. He brought with him a high-powered

team: Secretary of State Dean Rusk, Defense Secretary Robert
McNamara, Assistant Defense Secretary John McNaughton,
Chief Foreign Policy Adviser McGeorge Bundy, Agriculture
Secretary Orville Freeman, Health, Education and Welfare
Secretary John Gardner, Generals Earle Wheeler, William
Westmoreland, and Maxwell Taylor, Admiral U. S. Grant
Sharp, and Ambassadors Henry Cabot Lodge, Averell Harri-
man, and Leonard Unger.

I faced the president with General Thieu on one side of me
and General Nguyen Huu Co, my defense minister, on the
other.

President Johnson set the theme with the words: "We are
here to talk especially of the works of peace. We will leave
here determined not only to achieve victory over aggression,
but to win victory over hunger, disease, and despair. We are
making a reality out of the hopes of the common people."

His point was to proclaim that the United States was in
Vietnam not just to thwart the Communists but to help Vietnam defeat poverty and find its feet as a nation.

To develop this point, I pledged us to a social revolution,
an attack on ignorance and disease, and a goal of free self-
government. In a speech drafted on the plane to Honolulu, I
said, "I do not mean that we have to cure every one of our ills
before we go to the peace table, but we must have a record
of considerably more progress than we have been able to
accomplish so far. We must create a society that will be able
to withstand the false appeals of Communism. We must create
a society where each individual can feel that he has a future,
that he has respect and dignity, and that he has some chance
for himself and for his children to live in an atmosphere where
all is not disappointment, despair, and dejection." It was a
tough speech, not aggressive, but a forthright statement of my
dream of democracy in Vietnam.

Johnson listened carefully, and when I finished he leaned
forward and said, "Boy, you speak just like an American." From
him that was high praise.

I liked Johnson, we got on well together from the first, perhaps because both of us were men who got things done. For

instance, we were talking as we walked along one of the hotel corridors toward the conference room. I had suggested an improved TV network in Vietnam as a medium of information and propaganda. At that time we had only two mobile stations operating from airplanes. Johnson immediately turned to the group of aides following us and called out, "Where's the USIS man?" He told the official what I had said and added, "Premier Ky is right. Do something right now, please." Within a month the Americans had television in Vietnam. If my request had gone through normal channels it would have taken a couple of years.

Maxwell Taylor was also in Honolulu, but no longer as ambassador to Vietnam. The last time we met I had been a nobody in his book, and he had left me feeling angry and bitter. Now I was prime minister and talking face-to-face with the president while he was a back-room adviser.

I could sense his change in attitude because of the change in positions and I no longer felt antagonism. It is natural, I suppose, when you see a man who has been at the center of power but who now sits at the back of the room to forget everything that has passed and shake hands. That was what I did.

(And I was pleased to note that a week later Maxwell Taylor testified to the Senate Foreign Relations Committee that mine was "the first government which is solidly backed by the armed forces. As long as they are behind this government in the present sense, it is not going to be overturned by some noisy minority as some governments were overturned in the previous years. So I feel there is some encouragement, indicators of growing stability in the political scene.")

We issued a joint communiqué, which said: "The United States is pledged to the principle of the self-determination of peoples and of government by the consent of the governed. We have helped and we will help to stabilize the Vietnamese economy, to increase the production of goods, to spread the light of education and stamp out disease."

But the communiqué alone was not enough for Johnson. He gathered us all together on the final day. I can still see him stabbing his finger at each paragraph of the communiqué as he reviewed it point by point in his salty Texas style, glancing in turn at the appropriate minister and officials, making it clear to everyone beyond any doubt that he wanted not just words but action on building the new Vietnam. "Preserve this communiqué," he warned, "because it's one that we don't want to forget. It will be a kind of Bible that we are going to follow. When we come back here ninety days from now, or six months from now, we are going to start out and make reference to the announcements that the president, the chief of state, and the prime minister made.

"You men who are responsible for these departments, you ministers and the staffs associated with them in both governments, bear in mind we are going to give you an examination and the finals will be on just what you have done."

Turning to the problem of winning over the peasants, he asked, "How have you built democracy in the rural areas? How much of it have you built, when, and where? Give us dates, times, numbers.

"In paragraph two—'larger outputs, more efficient production to improve credit, handicraft, light industry, rural electrification.' Are those just phrases, high-sounding words, or have you coonskins on the wall?"

He turned to John Gardner, his Secretary of Health, Education and Welfare. "Next is health and education, Mr. Gardner. We don't want to talk about it; we want to do something about it: 'The president pledges he will dispatch teams of experts.' Well, we'd better do something besides dispatching. They should get out there. We are going to train health personnel. How many? You don't want to be like the fellow who was playing poker and when he made a big bet they called him and said, 'What have you got?' He said, 'Aces,' and they asked how many and he said, 'One ace.'

"Next is refugees. That is just as hot as a pistol in my country. You don't want me to raise a white flag and surrender, so we have to do something about that. . . ."

It was a remarkable performance. Only at the end did he touch on the subject of military power. "We haven't gone into the details of growing military effectiveness for two or three reasons. One, we want to be able honestly and truthfully to say that this has not been a military build-up conference here in Honolulu." And then, looking at me, he added a compliment, "We have been talking about building a society, following the outlines of the prime minister's speech yesterday."

On the final night of the conference, Johnson invited Thieu and me to his hotel suite with Westmoreland and one or two others. We had a few drinks, talked about nothing in particular, and then Johnson whispered to me: "Come into my bedroom for a moment."

I followed him, wondering what revelations were going to be unfolded in private. He closed the door, then asked: "I wondered if you would like to have an autographed picture of me." For a moment I thought that was all he had to say, but there was something else. He wondered if I would have any objection to Vice President Hubert Humphrey flying back with me in my plane next day to Vietnam. "I would like Humphrey to come with you and start the policy ball rolling, to get some action on the things we have talked about," he said.

"It's a good idea," I agreed. "But I didn't even know Mr. Humphrey was here."

"He isn't," Johnson said, with a grin. "But he will be by the time your plane takes off."

As soon as I left Johnson's bedroom, he telephoned Humphrey in Washington and asked him to catch the first flight to Honolulu, where he joined me.

Back home, I had two campaigns to fight: the first was against corruption and the black market; the second was to start a rural development program to make homes, if only temporary ones, for 280,000 refugees in pacified areas.

I traveled the country by helicopter, often accompanied by my wife, to meet the people and to let them see me. I had a completely open-door policy. Anyone, I said, could have access to the prime minister and, as far as I was able, I saw anyone.

A veteran with one leg, one arm, and one eye, living in the southern tip of Vietnam, heard about this and somehow made the trip to Saigon to call on me. The guards were horrified, but my aide was called and let him in. The man told me: "I can't get a job any more; the only thing I can hope for is to start a small business."

I asked him how much money he needed, but he did not know. "I'll give you 300,000 piastres," I said. He could hardly believe it. Then I added, "The trouble is, with all that money it is not safe for you to go back to your village by road," and I sent him home in my helicopter.

The day of the week did not matter if anyone wanted to see me. I slept so often at the "office," as I called the prime minister's house, that I rarely saw Mai and the children except on Sundays, when we all flew up to our equivalent of the American president's official country retreat at Camp David.

Ours was a magnificent, dazzling-white villa on spacious grounds, with a private beach, that had been built for the Emperor Bao Dai at Nha Trang, an hour's flight north of Saigon. It was called the White House. There we could all relax for one day a week—until the phone rang, as it did when Ambassador Lodge phoned me and said that an old friend of his, a Harvard professor, had arrived in Vietnam on a fact-finding tour and was anxious to talk with me. Could I spare him a little time? I knew I was going to be busy when I returned to Saigon, so, knowing that Lodge always had a plane at his disposal, I invited the two men to fly up for lunch.

They arrived at noon, and Lodge introduced the unknown professor before we had a pre-lunch cocktail. "This is Dr. Henry Kissinger," he said.

We ate a Vietnamese lunch, and Kissinger handled his chopsticks as easily as any problem he deals with. He put himself out to be charming to Mai, he played with the kids, and later we relaxed in deep, comfortable Western-style armchairs while he asked hundreds of questions, storing each answer in that remarkable brain of his, never taking a note.

My open-door policy extended even to Australia, where I made a state visit with my wife. The Australians were fighting magnificently in Vietnam, but there was much bitterness in Australia itself, and many people advised me not to make the visit. Even the wife of the Australian prime minister strongly opposed his inviting me. I refused to be put off, and in fact the Australian trip turned out to be one of the most successful I undertook.

I had to face a lot of criticism, and at one press conference a reporter from a Communist newspaper asked me if it was true that the Viet Cong controlled so much of South Vietnam that there was really no point in fighting any more.

"I don't have a map with me," I replied, "so I can't really give you a detailed answer. But if you really want to find out, you had better fly back with me to Vietnam and see for yourself."

"I accept that challenge," he shouted. And he did. He flew to Vietnam with me, in my own plane, and once there he was allowed to go anywhere he wanted. At the end of the week he came to thank me, and I heard later that back in Australia he told his "comrades" that they had been deceived. There were *some* rewarding moments in being prime minister.

There were tribulations too—some that could only be resolved by force. Particularly one.

8

THE BUDDHISTS:

Confrontation at Danang

In March 1966, barely a month after the Honolulu conference with President Johnson, I realized the time had come to have a showdown with the Buddhists, particularly their leader, Thich Tri Quang, whose attempts to control power from behind the scenes was seriously hampering the war effort.

The Buddhists had played a significant role in the downfall first of Diem, then of Khanh and Huong. Tri Quang, whose staring eyes and shining white teeth made such an impact on the TV screen, was an old campaigner in the art of stirring up trouble. He imagined himself to be a second Gandhi but in fact was nothing more than a politically motivated intriguer who thought that because I was only thirty-five, and not a professional politician, he would find it easy to manipulate me. He may also have believed that because I came from a Buddhist family, and had attacked Nhu for his viciousness toward the Buddhists, I would be putty in his hands. However, I was not going to be manipulated by anyone. My job was to try to win the war.

The Buddhists had grown more militant from the moment when Tri Quang emerged from the American embassy in Saigon where he had sought asylum after Nhu's purge of the pagodas. From his headquarters in Hue, he began the unification of the country's Buddhists. There were two main sects— the Mahayana (Greater Wheel), active in the center and North; and the Hinayana (Smaller Wheel), strong in the South. The differences between them were doctrinal, the Greater Wheel believing that it was open to all to attain the enlightenment of the Buddha, and the Smaller Wheel believing this was possible only for a few.

The Buddhists formed two new organizations: the High Clerical Association, which was doctrinal and headed by Tri Quang; and the Institute for the Propagation of the Buddhist Faith, which was secular and headed by Thich Tam Chau. These two were like the hard-man-and-soft-man teams of American and British detectives. Tri Quang was the hard man, issuing militant statements; Tam Chau was the soft man, adopting a more moderate line. The two alternated their pronouncements bewilderingly. Then they skillfully used the students, who had by now become something of a political force, making common cause with them, while the Viet Cong infiltrated agents to exploit student actions and encourage unrest.

Time after time I had meetings with the Buddhists, inviting a dozen or so at a time to my house, where I told them that I was not opposed to their aspirations, but that I realized they formed a large percentage of the population of Vietnam and had every right to be properly represented.

"I'm willing to discuss any problems you put forward," I said, "but if you believe in the destiny of South Vietnam, if you want us to survive against Communism, which is an enemy of your religion, surely it's time we united against the common foe. What I can't understand is why you have to organize demonstrations, cause trouble, and generally weaken our cause against Communism."

The Buddhists had asked for free elections. "I'm going to give you free elections," I promised them. "I have already given my word. So why do you try to force me out of office when I have promised to do what you want?"

I told the Buddhist leaders that if they could overthrow me in a free election I would be the first to recognize the decision, but I added, "I can assure you of one thing. If you choose the way of the sword to take over, I will not hesitate to kill every Buddhist leader before I relinquish office."

The Buddhists were trying to cut South Vietnam in two— and they nearly succeeded where the Viet Cong failed. Since a

Buddhist bonze cannot hold power, all the Buddhist leaders could hope for was to make certain that their puppet would respond to the strings they pulled.

The naïveté of the Buddhist leaders was pathetic. As the crisis deepened, Tri Quang went to see Henry Cabot Lodge, the American ambassador, and told him he was determined to overthrow me. As Lodge recounted the incident to me, he asked Tri Quang, "But just suppose you do overthrow Marshal Ky. Who would you choose to replace him as prime minister?"

Tri Quang sat quietly for a moment, thinking hard. Then he made the astounding observation to Lodge, "We will be willing to put Marshal Ky back." All that Tri Quang wanted was to prove that *he* was the power behind the throne.

By March 1966 demonstrations were breaking out in many major cities, particularly in the Buddhist strongholds of Hue and Danang. Even worse, there were confirmed reports that many troops in First Corps, stationed in that area, might refuse to fight against the Buddhists if it came to a showdown. It seemed incredible that at a time when every effort should have been directed to attacking Communism, we were actually facing the possibility of military revolt.

First Corps was under the command of General Nguyen Chan Thi, himself a Buddhist, and a man I had been watching carefully for some time. Coming from peasant stock, Thi was a man who excited either admiration or dislike. There was no middle way. I have no doubt in my mind that he was actively using the Buddhists to promote his own power. Many people also believed that he had picked up left-wing inclinations in Cambodia, where he had fled after plotting unsuccessfully against Diem in 1960, and taken a mistress who was believed to be a Communist. Thi was a born intriguer. He played a serious role in bringing Khanh to power and then helped to kick him out.

Yet I had to tread carefully. I was prime minister of Vietnam, not a dictator. I could not make all the decisions, I could only try to carry out the decrees of our government. As I told *Time* magazine, "Governing a country like South Vietnam is a very delicate matter, requiring balance. The way we work is that my colleagues and I decide what we want done, and then I try to carry it out."

This was a deliberate policy. When I became prime minister I decided that the commanders of each of the four army corps must be kept fully informed of all policy decisions—and Thi was one of those commanders. I picked them personally on a basis of true friendship.

Now, apparently, Thi was nursing ambitions to become an old-fashioned warlord, for I was receiving daily proof that instead of helping to maintain order in the highly sensitive Hue–Danang area, he was helping the Buddhists. So I decided that he must go. I flew to Danang and dismissed him, though I softened the blow by an announcement that he had resigned his command because of health reasons and would shortly leave for the United States for medical treatment. In fact he chose not to go and remained under discreet house arrest for some time.

As this was happening I announced publicly that a new constitution would be drafted as soon as possible, to be followed by general elections. I was willing to hold any necessary referendums on the new constitution.

In March I called a meeting of the Directorate (the National Leadership Committee) and the Armed Forces Council and promised to convene a national political convention in which even the poorest of the land would be represented—in fact, particularly the poorest. At the press conference that followed, I denied that any of us wanted to cling to power, and promised categorically, "I will resign tomorrow if my resignation will help to restore stability." Why not? My heart was in flying, not in politics, into which I had stumbled almost by accident.

The Americans backed my action and my plans. Ambassador Lodge realized that I had no option but to strengthen the government by getting rid of dissident elements, even when the Buddhists appealed directly to President Johnson. Wisely Johnson ignored their pleas. After all, the Americans were, by the spring of 1966, making vital decisions, far more important than internal Vietnamese problems. General Maxwell Taylor was proposing that Haiphong should be mined. I knew that within days the United States Air Force would start regular B-52 bombing raids on North Vietnam, and that by now America had nearly a quarter of a million troops in Vietnam, together with another 50,000 naval forces in the area. And Westmoreland was asking for still more men.

The very proper refusal of the United States to interfere in the internal affairs of South Vietnam provoked an inevitable anti-American backlash among the Buddhists. Soon I was branded as an "American stooge" and the walls of many cities were daubed with that well-known phrase "Yanks go home!"

The demonstrations that followed General Thi's dismissal caused deep unease in Washington, based on a fear that I would be overthrown and replaced by a neutralist Buddhist government. Five hastily convened crisis meetings were held at the White House between April 9 and 20 at which members of the administration reviewed options open to America.

The two chief ones were Option A, presented by George Carver, a CIA analyst, which favored continuing the American commitment unchanged, and Option C, argued by Under Secretary of State George W. Ball, which called for disengagement from Vietnam. Ball declared: "We should concentrate our attention on cutting our losses. . . . There are no really attractive options open to us."

In Option B, Deputy Assistant Secretary of State Leonard Unger favored continuing the war but seeking a compromise settlement, and in Option BP, Assistant Secretary of Defense John McNaughton recommended continuing the war "with a pessimistic outlook."

The decision, insofar as there was any decision, was to make no change in the policy. William Bundy, Assistant Secretary of State for Far Eastern Affairs, despite being in favor of continuation, warned prophetically: "The war could well become an albatross around the administration's neck at least equal to what Korea was for President Truman in 1952."

Back in Saigon the tension mounted. Daily demonstrations in Saigon and Chinese Cholon took different forms. One day tough youngsters of the Buddhist Youth Movement, distinguished by their white shirts, would go on the rampage, over-turning any unattended American automobiles or jeeps in sight, stoning windows. The next day the demonstrators would play a quieter role: perhaps 2,000 people would sit patiently for three hours in front of the Vinh Hoa Dao pagoda, listening to speeches, the violence barely hidden beneath the surface.

In Hue the bonzes walked in sedate torchlight processions over the Perfume River bridge, while the younger ones sought to prove that Hue was the heart of the "struggle movement" by seizing the radio station and staging a sit-in at the university. Many soldiers openly sided with them, even General Nhuan, commander of the First Army Division.

Not the least perplexed were the American advisers in the central region, who suddenly found themselves advising soldiers determined to bring down the government which the Americans were committed to support. Understandably the Americans were angry. Here they were spending vast sums of money, time, sweat, and blood, in order to help save a country from Communism, and what thanks did they get? Abuse, disloyalty, and before long their own USIS buildings reduced to ashes by arson. Throughout the late spring the hatred for all things American continued and reputable columnists like Cyrus L. Sulzberger, who came to see me in Saigon at the time, wrote in *The New York Times* that the Viet Cong were so deeply infiltrated into the Buddhist movement that Danang and Hue would fall unless something were done. Like two roads meeting, the Buddhists and Communists were now treading the same path, thanks to skillful Communist exploitation of Buddhist disturbances.

Tri Quang even had the effrontery to boast that if the Buddhists continued their anti-American demonstrations, the United States troops might quit. Wearing his well-known "Gandhi smile," this pseudo-pious humbug added, "And if the Americans do leave I will have achieved passively what the Viet Cong have been unable to do by killing people."

Words were bad enough. But suddenly I received proof that many Buddhists were heavily armed, especially the "Death Volunteers," who, ironically, were using American rifles. They acquired them simply by enlisting for a training period at some local camp, then bolting with their equipment.

I felt, with Sulzberger, that the cancer was spreading so rapidly that the only hope of saving the patient—the government—lay in surgery, in cutting out the cancer at the source. I decided to do just this and prepared plans to "liberate" Danang.

I faced one fundamental question: Should I inform the Americans of my intention? I did not make the decision lightly, but in the end I decided to act in secret.

The United States government did not always understand the Buddhist problem in Vietnam or for that matter the forces motivating other warring factions in the country, either political, social, or religious. Their ignorance derived from their anxiety not to pry too deeply into our internal affairs for fear of giving the appearance of being a colonial power, but I felt that sometimes they held back too much, that a little more expert knowledge might have helped us all. Even in the American embassy in Saigon, only two men—and they were both young —were concerned with the political aspects of our struggle.

All in all, I decided to go it alone. I did not consult the Americans at this time, for Lodge had already told me, before leaving for the United States, that in general terms the White House was convinced that if I could establish a policy of firmness it would help the war effort. It was my understanding, without any question whatsoever, that America wanted a government that had real authority to back up the huge commitment America itself was making.

Yet I still hoped the Buddhists would see reason. Unfortunately, men like Tri Quang, remembering their past successes against politicians, completely misread my character. Believing that I was inexperienced, they were convinced they could master me. But it was precisely the fact that I was not a professional politician that gave me added strength. I was a military man in every sense of the word (I had known no other life since school) and to me it was normal to consecrate my life to the fatherland without thought of politics and self-interest. And so when I did hesitate to take action, the Buddhists misinterpreted my reluctance as political weakness and built up further pressures on the central government.

Soon I realized the time had come to act. One army division had virtually joined the Buddhists. So had Special Zone forces in Quang Nam and Quang Da. I knew that if this trend continued, even for two weeks longer, the whole of the central area would fall into Buddhist hands and be proclaimed an autonomous territory. Already the radio station, municipal buildings, and army HQ in Danang were in Buddhist hands. Already the insurgents were using Communist guerrilla methods of infiltration, distributing weapons to the people of Danang, dividing the populace into groups and committees, each group spying on the others. An order had been issued forbidding anyone in Danang to listen to Saigon radio. In other words, Danang was almost like a Communist-occupied city. So at 3 A.M. on May 14 I held a top-level conference with my military chiefs to put my plans into action. It was so secret that I did not even tell President Thieu, let alone the Americans. At 5 A.M., troops, supported by my own wing of fighter-bombers, flew into Danang. I sent the head of our Joint General Staff as commander of the operation. With some regret I felt that my place must be in the prime minister's office in Saigon.

At first there was little opposition. We used paratroops, marines, and tanks in a commando-type assault. The element of surprise was so complete that we seized the radio station and other key points almost before the dissidents had time to wake up. My main objective was not the civilian section of the city, but the army headquarters, which had openly sided with the Buddhists. Soon we ran into a problem: an American problem.

It is not difficult to imagine the consternation among the Americans in Danang. They had been advising Vietnamese troops, who were now attacked by other Vietnamese troops. Ignorant of the problem behind the action, they asked themselves whom they should support. The United States Marines at Danang were commanded by General Lewis W. Walt, who was also adviser to First Corps. He was furious at an assault without warning on what he regarded as his territory.

Some pro-Buddhist troops of First Corps had actually trained their artillery on the Danang air base when our aircraft landed, and threatened to open fire. Anxious to avoid bloodshed I phoned Danang, and ordered one plane to fly over the artillery compound with a message written on paper and dropped from an airplane: "If you fire one single round, I will destroy every gun in the artillery base." They knew I would keep my word, and there was no artillery fire.

However, the sight of that aircraft—however peaceful the mission—infuriated General Walt, for soon afterward the head of our Joint General Staff phoned from Danang to my office in Saigon. His message was terse and to the point: "General Walt has asked me to stop the operation," he said. "If we continue to use air cover, he has threatened to send American planes into the air to shoot ours down."

At this point I contacted Ambassador Lodge, and told him of General Walt's threat, adding, "I must ask you if this is the policy of your government. If it is true, then I am going to fly up to Danang in ten minutes and lead the planes in action, just to see if the Americans have the courage to shoot down the prime minister of Vietnam."

Lodge could hardly believe what I told him and promised to send a message immediately to Walt. Even so, the Vietnamese commander on the spot still asked me to fly up, so around lunch time I flew to Danang to review the situation. I told my local commanders to line up our biggest guns and train them directly at the American base on the other side of the small river. "If Americans start to shoot down our planes," I said, "destroy the marine base. That is an order."

I had hardly finished when General Walt sent a message asking me to come and see him; presumably he had heard from the American embassy in Saigon. I said I was sorry, I had no time to spare. A few minutes later Walt repeated his request, this time with more insistence. Again I said "No." Finally Walt sent a message, "Then can I come to see you?"

I sent a message back, "No, sorry, I'm just too busy."

Finally Walt sent a message that he had received instructions from Washington to talk to me before I left Danang. Though I was furious at his attitude, I felt this farce had gone on long enough and perhaps, since I was in the driver's seat, I could afford to be magnanimous. "All right," I replied, "I can spare you five minutes."

There was no question of my going to see Walt. He came to my small office on the Danang air base with the American consul to Danang, a man who had openly sided with the Buddhists. Walt saluted very correctly, after which I asked him, "What can I do for you, General? What do you want?"

"Why did you send troops in here?" asked Walt.

"Is it really any business of yours, General?" I asked.

"Well, I'm in command of the American marines here, and I'm the adviser to the Vietnamese Command. I think in view of my position I might have been told what was happening."

"In normal military operations, perhaps, General," I replied, "but not in this kind of operation. This is an internal problem—the people versus the government. If I may speak frankly, it's none of your business and you don't have to know about it. Tell me, General, how many years have you served in the American army?"

Slightly taken aback, Walt said he had been twenty-three years in the armed forces.

"Well," I replied, "having been in the military hierarchy that long, you ought to know that sometimes an officer receives orders from his commander in chief before an operation starts, sometimes during an operation, and sometimes after. That is true, isn't it?"

When he nodded, I added, "If I feel that you need to know anything about a military operation, of course I will let you know; but that has nothing to do with the present case."

Walt persisted, "But you know Danang is quiet. My marines can go out into the bars for a drink. I don't see why you had to send in troops."

"That's your opinion, General, not mine. I'm delighted your marines can go out and have a drink, but that has nothing to do with what I'm trying to do, which is to restore the authority of the central government. Suppose a unit under your command rebelled against your authority? Would you tolerate it?"

I knew his answer would be "No."

"Well, now that you are here, General, let me tell you something. We have a government in Saigon. I am the prime minister. If the Buddhists in this area try to overthrow the government, I'm in the same position as you would be if you had to restore order against a rebellion."

Walt was now quieter, more understanding, though he asked me a little apprehensively whether I was going to launch an attack on Hue. I told him I was not. He seemed very relieved. I had already made my plans for Hue. To me the coastline of this area resembled a snake, with Hue the head, Danang the body, and the pro-Buddhist provinces of Quang Tin and Quang Nam, south of Danang, the tail. I did not want to kill the snake, which I could have done if I had attacked Hue, the head. So I had attacked the body—Danang, a port, less emotionally involved than Hue—in order to paralyze the snake. Now I planned to blockade north and south of Danang. To me this seemed a perfect example of combining politics and military tactics, and I felt later that, though my standing with Johnson was already excellent, this was the moment when the American leaders really began to have more confidence in me and to back me more seriously.

When Lodge returned to Saigon on May 20 he seemed very satisfied with the outcome. Lodge was the sort of good diplomat who, whatever his feelings, never presumed to give advice, and was the essence of tact. But on this occasion he did tell me, "I'm delighted you took the decision to send in troops. If you hadn't you'd have disappointed me."

As so often happens, I later became good friends with General Walt and when I visited the Danang area he sometimes flew with me in my helicopter to lonely outposts. Often I would return to his headquarters for lunch. On one occasion I told him how pleased I was to see Tabasco sauce on the table. It was my favorite sauce.

"Well," he said, "the man who bottles it back home is one

of my best friends and I'll see you're never short of Tabasco as long as you live."

Indeed he did. Walt arranged for a case of Tabasco to be sent to me every month. But Tabasco has to be taken in moderation, and I must have left a dozen cases in Saigon after the fall of South Vietnam.

Hue presented no problems, as I had expected. We cut all the roads leading from Danang, the nearest port to Hue, so that no gasoline, food, or supplies could get through. The ancient capital, controlled by Tri Quang and General Nhuan, surrendered soon afterward and only then did I send in police troops to keep order.

Tri Quang was flown to Saigon, though we had quite a problem in getting this politically minded monk into the aircraft, for, as the pilot told me, when Tri Quang heard the plane would be flying over the sea on its way to Saigon, he became convinced he was only being put on board so we could dump him into the water.

I had to be careful with Tri Quang since I did not want to create a martyr, so I decided on a compromise, and confined him to house arrest in a Saigon hospital. Knowing the sort of tricks he would be up to, I deliberately chose a hospital in which one of the doctors was a friend of Tri Quang's. Tri Quang stayed in the hospital "recuperating" for several months but almost immediately on entering it announced that he was going on a hunger strike.

Just what I expected. But, despite all the newspaper stories of his impending death, Tri Quang never seemed to lose weight. Each time the American advisers asked me when he would die, I replied, "If he were a real Buddhist priest, then perhaps he *would* die, but Tri Quang is a politician and his doctor friend is feeding him secretly. Don't worry, for a politician death is the end. Tri Quang must survive if he wants to carry on his political career."

Things quieted down after I had quelled the Buddhists, and I was able to get on with the business of government. It was (and always has been) my earnest belief that, given stability, civilian rule is infinitely preferable to that of a military junta, and by May 1966 I was able to sign a decree setting up a committee to draft electoral laws and procedures. I announced that my government would stay in power for at least another year to see the task completed. The following month I signed another decree setting September 11 as the date for the election of a constituent assembly as the first step toward a civilian government.

Provincial chiefs presented a list of names, and 117 delegates, representing all political, religious, and racial groups, with one representative for every 50,000 people, were chosen in a free election. They met in October in the Assembly building in Saigon and discussed various issues before settling to the first real task I had for them—the writing of a constitution.

It was completed in March 1967 and provided for a president with wide powers and a prime minister and cabinet responsible to a two-chamber House. It included a bill of rights, provision for the encouragement of labor unions and land reform, and improvement in the welfare of the peasants.

It met with widespread approval; indeed, President Johnson said later that he had looked at it "just as proudly as I looked at Lynda, my first baby."

In May 1967 we held local elections in 4,612 hamlets and in October there were elections for the lower House, resulting in reasonable representation for the military, the government bureaucrats, and the Buddhists.

And all this was done against the background of the war. In June 1967 I called for a force of 600,000 American troops to match our own South Vietnamese forces. At that time the American strength was something over 450,000.

Robert McNamara visited South Vietnam to assess the scene and Westmoreland suggested another 70,000 troops. McNamara, however, wanted to keep any increase to a minimum. The two of them reported to the president, who promised that troops would be supplied as necessary. But first he sent General Taylor and Clark Clifford on a tour of the Far East to seek more third-power forces.

I promised them that we would increase the South Vietnamese forces to 685,000, though Thieu was reluctant to go beyond this for fear of disrupting the economy, and in August Johnson promised 40,000 to 50,000 more troops to bring the American contingent up to half a million.

President Johnson and I got on well together, though I was sorry that on one occasion, when we held a conference at Guam, he—or his advisers—refused to implement an idea I put forward. It was a simple, bold plan. I wanted to send South Vietnamese troops across the border into Ho Chi Minh territory and set up a base in North Vietnam. If the Communists could establish a stronghold in the South, there was no reason why the South Vietnamese could not build a secure base in the North. With such a base we could mobilize anti-Communists in the North, and become a strategic thorn to the Communists, who considered North Vietnam a secure base from which to send their troops and supplies to attack us. I volunteered to parachute down into North Vietnam and command the base. Regrettably, President Johnson said "No"; and the Vietnamese armed forces did not have the capability to sustain such a base without American support and supplies.

It was a great pity, but otherwise, we seemed to be on the way to victory.

9

CORRUPTION:

The PX millionaires

I passed up a chance to become a millionaire overnight when I rejected the advances of a Japanese automobile firm that wanted to establish a factory in Vietnam. There was nothing unlawful about the proposal. We already had automobiles being made under license and as prime minister I was approached regularly by foreign companies hoping to set up factories. My own concern was to choose the best companies and the best deals for Vietnam.

The Japanese employed a Buddhist monk as a go-between and he came to see me and my wife at home. After a little preliminary skirmishing he came out with a breathtaking offer: if I signed I would get $1 million for myself in cash and three hundred automobiles to distribute to my friends.

When I turned down the monk's offer out of hand Mai kicked me sharply beneath the table. "I'm not suggesting you should have accepted," she said later, "but you can't say no right away to such a fantastic proposition. You should have taken time to think."

I told her, "I don't agree. I'm human, like the next man, and time might lead to temptation."

Corruption was one of Vietnam's biggest problems and one against which I campaigned. In the winter of 1965-6 I launched an anti-corruption drive, during the course of which I had a crooked Chinese businessman named Ta Vinh publicly executed by a firing squad in Saigon's central market.

Ta Vinh was in the steel black market and after the passing of sentence, but before the execution, I was inundated with pleas—backed by heavy bribes—to change my mind. They did not come from his family, but diplomats and top-ranking businessmen, men of power and influence. Because I refused to change my mind, some powerful businessmen realized that I always backed my words with actions, and at least that tended to curb the black market.

The black market in rice was an even greater scandal—for rice touched the bellies of everyone—and I immediately set about stamping it out. The rice-trading system in Vietnam lay in the hands of ten moguls, most of them Chinese. They could arrange any price they liked. They had started to hoard rice, and when I began government searches I discovered that they even dumped rice in the river to create a scarcity in the market, resulting in skyrocketing prices and a spiraling cost of living which (they hoped) would bring down my government so that, with a new government, they could continue their wicked trade.

I ordered the ten businessmen to report to my office, and without giving them a chance to speak, I lined them up in front of my desk and told them: "I am perfectly aware of your intention to try to overthrow the government by dumping rice. Now let me tell you something. If I fall, you won't stay alive."

As they watched I wrote down their names on ten pieces of paper and put them in my cap.

"I'll give you one week to re-supply the market with enough rice at a reasonable and stable price," I warned them. "If you cannot do this by the deadline, I shall draw lots and the first man whose name I pick out of my cap will be shot. At the end of the second week, if my ultimatum is still not satisfied, I shall draw a second name out of my cap and that man will be shot; and I shall do this until there is enough rice for everyone."

The result of this undemocratic approach was astounding: within three days the markets were filled with rice and its price was frozen.

I faced similar problems in the gold market. There was such a panic in gold speculation, and so much hoarding, that gold disappeared. I suggested to the Treasury that we should sell gold in the open market so the price of gold would fall. The minister of economics said it was impossible. No government had ever taken such a step; and apart from this, our gold came from the United States and the Americans might not allow us to sell it openly. "We won't actually sell it," I replied. "Here's what we'll do instead." I instructed subordinates to spread rumors that the government was going to sell gold to the people at one of the biggest jewelry stores in Saigon. Within twenty-four hours the gold price was stabilized. All one really needed was a good idea, the right propaganda at the right moment.

Of course it was uphill work, for by the time I took office corruption, black marketeering, and crime were firmly rooted in South Vietnam. There had been some corruption under the French, but for every minor French official who took a bribe there were probably ten Vietnamese taking them after the French left. If anyone wanted a permit or a license, money changed hands. Eventually even hotel managers expected a bribe before accepting a reservation.

After the French came the Americans—and the black marketeering flourished as never before. This is no criticism of the Americans; it is an inevitable fact of life when thousands of foreign troops pour into a country, especially when they are GIs earning more in a week than a Vietnamese might earn in a year.

Every American army unit had a PX and every PX was a treasure trove of luxury goods that could turn the unscrupulous into PX millionaires. Any American soldier buying a duty-free article from a PX could quadruple his money by re-selling it, and then what happened? Members of my anti-corruption squad actually traced the history of a refrigerator bought from the PX by a GI and then sold illegally, for five times the price he paid, to a Vietnamese. It passed through ten different pairs of hands before finally reposing in the kitchen of a Vietnamese general's girl friend.

No one could control the black market. Prices rocketed, yet thousands of ordinary Vietnamese were sitting behind desks earning the same salaries they had received before inflation started running at 30 percent a year. The clerk's salary was never raised to match the black market prices and so he had to find the extra money from other sources. If he could not get into the black market himself, then, in order to live, he solicited bribes.

After all, he had seen men at the top lining their bank accounts. For though Diem had been an honest man who passed a law recommending the death penalty for corruption, he was too out of touch to see what was going on. Nepotism is a form of corruption, and his relatives were everywhere, and they were unscrupulous. While one brother, Ngo Dinh Nhu, was in charge of security he obtained government funds to finance his Can Lao party and was involved in extortion rackets and opium smuggling. Another brother, Archbishop Ngo Dinh Thuc, obtained funds for the Catholic clergy. A third brother, Ngo Dinh Can, made a fortune by controlling many shipping concessions and part of the cinnamon trade. Diem made his youngest brother ambassador to London and Madame Nhu's father ambassador to Washington. What examples for poverty-stricken clerks and soldiers!

Inevitably the slime of corruption oozed into every crevice of our lives, often without the country's leaders realizing its extent. I was shattered one day when a woman who had lived near my family in Son Tay in the North came to see me in the prime minister's office. Her husband had been a sergeant in my first platoon, but as I hardly knew the family I had never seen him since those far-off days. She told me that he had been killed in action two years previously, and hesitantly said that she was applying to her local state bank for a loan, and since I had known her husband could she use my name as a reference.

Since the widows or children of men killed in action received cash lump sums to tide them over, I asked, without thinking, "Have you spent all your compensation money?"

"No, Sir," she said eagerly, "that's what I want the loan for."

What she said was nonsense and rather sharply I told her so. "What did you do with your compensation?"

"I never had it, Sir," she replied. "I've tried for two years!" She hesitated and added, "I *could* have it next week if . . ."

"Well, then . . ." I began.

"If I give a member of our local tribunal half of it."

I was shocked and horrified and I followed that case through to the source. Every word was true. Even worse, I uncovered cases where widows of heroes who had died in the service of our country had actually sold their children in order to live, because their compensation payments had been held back. Of course I cleaned out this nest of corrupt vipers, but how can one man search for the dust that is swept under a carpet covering the entire country?

Corruption touched every family—and even I had to be careful. When I succeeded Quat as premier, I discovered that Quat's secretary, whom I would normally inherit, was a nephew of mine. I transferred him immediately, for I was determined to be the first prime minister who did not have one single relative in any government post, and the first premier whose wife and relatives would never be involved in any illegal business. I succeeded in that, though sometimes problems were unexpected, as in the case of Mai's stepbrother, who was waiting to be drafted. Her mother wanted to send the boy to Paris to complete his education in safety. The family dared not approach me because they knew I would refuse to help, so they bribed the mistress of my minister of the interior, paying a million piastres ($10,000) for a false passport.

Unfortunately for the boy, he could not get a visa for France, so he tried to get there via Cambodia, failed to bribe the Cambodians, and landed in jail. At this point Mai's relatives came to me. I told them: "It is better that he stays in jail. He is safe there and this will be a lesson for you."

Many of the wives of men in power were unable to resist the temptation of bribery if they could persuade their husbands to help a friend, particularly when it came to conscription, where at one stage the price of 100,000 piastres for preventing a friend's son from being drafted was so common that women playing poker for high stakes often cried, "I'll raise you a soldier."

I knew of one general's wife who took no money for keeping a young man out of the army. He was her hairdresser, and was at her beck and call throughout the war.

Nowhere was draft-dodging more widespread than in Cholon, adjacent to Saigon. With a population that was 90 percent Chinese, no one in Cholon had any desire to fight, and most fathers paid heavy bribes to keep their sons from being drafted. Over 100,000 in Cholon dodged the draft. But the price was high. And it all went to the chief of police.

In the days of the Young Turks my flying colleagues used to joke, "Ky, if you ever become premier and you want to find jobs for your old pals, don't bother to make us cabinet ministers, just make one of us the chief of police of Precinct Five." Precinct Five was in Cholon and to become chief of police, a man often had to pay a bribe of 15 million piastres to the right contact, but he knew he could triple that sum within two years.

Bribery became so open that people were sometimes astonished when they found it was unnecessary. After the Diem coup, some property of the Catholic Church was confiscated; I signed a deed that restored it while waiting in an airport lounge before leaving on a state visit to Malaysia. But at the same time many government contractors had their fortunes frozen. Some of them were crooks, but the honest suffered with the guilty.

The wife of one contractor came to Mai and offered $100,000 if I could be induced to sign a decree unlocking her husband's money. I checked, found there was no serious evidence of misappropriation by the woman or her husband, and did as she asked. She could barely believe it when I declined the pay-off.

Money from bribes found its way into the pockets and purses of bar girls, pimps, beggars, blackmailers, and that curse of society, the drug peddler. The drug problem was behind much of the corruption. Heroin was readily available in South Vietnam; it was cheap and of high quality.

Most of the opium from which it was made was grown in Burma, the rest in northern Laos. The refining center was Vientiane, from where it was flown to Saigon, often in Coca-Cola cans. Some was air-dropped from Laotian or Vietnamese military aircraft, but much was landed at Saigon airport.

The Americans dared not tackle the problem at the Laotian end because they feared an open breach with Laos; they were incapable of curbing the traffic at the Saigon end, where customs inspectors were bribed to turn a blind eye to it. At one time two of the key customs posts were held by brothers of Prime Minister Khiem, and the government took the view that it was an American problem.

So opium was sold openly in the streets of Saigon and around the American bases. It was cheap compared to prices in the United States and, since it was white, pure, and adulterated very little on its short journey (compared to the product sold in America and Europe), it was highly prized by those who had already developed a habit.

In the disciplined force of American troops that had first arrived in South Vietnam, the problem might have been restricted to a few, but by the early seventies U.S. Command estimated that 10 percent of the troops in Vietnam were taking heroin and 5 percent were addicts.

American morale had slumped. Many troops were draftees with little desire to fight and risk death in a war they no longer cared about. Some were openly against the war and took to wearing peace symbols. All were affected to some degree by the changing attitude to the war back home, and by the growth of the hippie movement in the United States.

After the My Lai massacre disclosures the army's stock slumped even lower; the GI began to feel like a leper. More and more men opted out, taking to pot and retreating into a drugged dream world. Sometimes unsympathetic disciplinarians were "fragged" with grenades, and as a result officers became reluctant to give direct orders.

Dope, and the changed climate of opinion back home, led to disintegration of morale in a mighty army. And that was not the end of the story. GIs took the habit back to America, and the drug problem, already a cause for concern, became more acute there. It was as if the Vietnamese had taken a terrible revenge on their patronizing guests and given them a social disease as infectious as a venereal one.

Virtually anything and everything was available in Vietnam at a price. Much of what was on sale was stolen. In 1967,

according to American officials, a total of half a million tons
of rice was stolen. Merchandise from American and Vietnamese
army supplies, consignments of refrigerators, TV sets, motor-
cycles, all were stolen. Entire convoy loads of beer and wristwatches, typewriters and fire extinguishers were hijacked. Out
of sixty-eight truckloads of cement imported at one time in
1967, forty-two were stolen. When Saigon imported forty
garbage trucks to help clean its littered streets, many were
stolen at the docks. One Vietnamese truck driver toured Saigon
for two days in 1967 trying vainly to find a buyer for a stolen
computer worth $2.5 million. In Qui Nhon market you could
buy anything from army rations and clothing to washing machines and grenades. Weapons changed hands at $25 to $30
apiece and if you wanted to buy a tank or a helicopter it could
be arranged.

To help restrain inflation the United States Army issued
script instead of dollars to soldiers. In 1970 an entire container
truck loaded with tons of script with a face value of millions
was stolen at Saigon airport.

In 1971 a U.S. Senate subcommittee found that one single
American contractor lost $118 million in a year through pilfer-
ing. The total loss to the U.S. government through illegal currency rackets was officially and conservatively put at a half
billion dollars a year.

Theft was not the only problem. There were widespread
irregularities in fulfilling contracts. While I was prime minister
I discovered that the quantity of pharmaceuticals—particularly
antibiotics—supposed to have been delivered by America would
have been sufficient to cope with the requirements of all Asia;
and the amount of cement allegedly delivered could have
turned the whole of Vietnam into a concrete platform. This
was not a question of theft or maladministration. Much of it
never arrived.

A United States government committee (in August 1967)
uncovered kickbacks in all commodity fields and evidence of
scores of transactions such as the one in which a United States
company invoiced a commodity at $10,000, but shipped goods
worth about $700.

I also had to fight a black market in the currency. By 1970 the official exchange rate had reached 118 piastres to the dollar, but on the black market the Indian and Chinese money changers offered 500 piastres to the dollar. Men with suitcases stuffed with currency flew in on almost every plane. An American Senate subcommittee estimated that at least $500 million changed hands illicitly in a year.

Later in 1970 America and Vietnam agreed on a new rate of exchange for Americans who were entitled to change dollars. It was a more realistic 275 piastres to the dollar, but it was not sufficient to kill the black-market deals.

With crime and corruption so rampant, it was impossible to keep even the armed forces honest. General Van Toan, commander of the Second Vietnamese Division while I was prime minister in 1966, was known as the Cinnamon General because of the fortune he had made from stealing that valuable spice. His division was stationed in a mountainous area south of Danang famous for its cinnamon trees and I soon heard that Toan was peddling cinnamon in the black market, cinnamon that he collected by sending out troops with vehicles intended for operations.

I confronted Toan at Danang and demanded, "Is it true?" He admitted that it was, but insisted that he was not trading for his personal benefit. He said: "Our troops have not got enough money. Neither have I, for that matter. But I did it for the social welfare of the troops." And he claimed that he had made only 1,300 piastres (about $13 at that time).

He was lying, of course, but Toan was not a real crook. He had more guts than most and was always in the front line when needed. So I told him: "If you and your men need more money, then your duty is to come to see me and I will try to do something about it. But the cinnamon traffic stops now, and if I hear one more word about it you will be court-martialed."

I put the Cinnamon General "on probation," but I had no compunction in dismissing my defense minister, General Nguyen Huu Co, for corruption. He could never have lived the way he did on his official pay; he had twelve children and a liking for champagne and women. His racket was real estate.

Co bought barren land which he later disposed of to the United States purchasing authority as sites for American installations. He also drew three million piastres a year in rent from the Americans for government land at Nha Trang.

Co and I had worked together as Young Turks. He had accompanied me to the Honolulu conference with President Johnson in 1966, but when I discovered the full extent of his dealings I fired him. He was out of the country at the time, on one of his regular visits to Taiwan, and I sent him a cable telling him not to return. He settled down to live in exile in Hong Kong, though I heard that he developed a line of correspondence courses, advising other generals remaining in Vietnam on their business activities.

Many of the generals had side interests. The most famous was General Dang Van Quang of Fourth Corps who traded in opium and rice.

When I discovered that Quang dealt in the black market, that he was spiriting goods into Cambodia, I decided to fire him. According to law Thieu, as head of the Armed Forces Council, had to sign the decree. When I proposed to the AFC that Quang should be dismissed, Thieu knew that if the AFC agreed with me and he refused to sign, there would be an immediate reaction. So Thieu signed. But later Thieu took Quang back as one of his right-hand men, and Quang made a fortune, most of which he stashed away in Switzerland. As special assistant to Thieu in charge of security, he handled all passport and exit visa problems. Before long he was charging $5,000 for a passport. When the rush to leave became a rout, he upped the price of a passport to $20,000. Anyone who needed a passport—even for the wives and children of senators and judges—had to pay Quang.

Thieu gave little encouragement to my efforts to stamp out corruption, though in 1972 he got rid of another defense minister, General Nguyen Van Vy, as a result of a scandal involving the misappropriation of army savings funds.

Corruption went on seething, the subject of open gossip and condemnation but virtually unchecked until 1974 when the growth was lanced by an upsurge of public indignation, and then there were mass firings and the president himself stood accused.

It began in April 1974 when our Senate held an inquiry into a racket in imported fertilizers. Its report at the end of June showed that more than 70 percent of imported fertilizers, financed by American aid, had been hoarded and then resold to peasants for at least double the official price. (Now I knew why no one backed my efforts to manufacture our own fertilizers!) Huge profits had been made. The report named sixty businessmen who had been involved and recommended the dismissal of Nguyen Duc Cuong, the minister of trade and industry, all his senior officials, and ten provincial chiefs.

Curiously, the first repercussion of the inquiry came when Thieu dismissed Nguyen Van Ngan, one of his closest aides and organizer of the Democratic Party, the Dan Chu Dang. It happened even before the inquiry reported and, though no reason was stated, it was widely thought that Ngan was punished for supporting the inquiry, for it was rumored that Madame Thieu's family was involved.

The report was followed by a call for more action against corruption. A conference of three hundred Catholic priests in June founded the People's Anti-Corruption Movement. The clergy, who included parish priests, teachers, and chaplains, signed a declaration accusing "government mafias" of speculating in fertilizers, rice, insecticides, pharmaceutical products, and raw materials "in order to plunder the people and enrich the wealthy."

It went on: "Corruption is making all the nation's constructive efforts useless, undermining all programs for national development and destroying all the people's confidence in their leaders. Under the protection of powerful officials, the drug traffic, organized crime, gambling, prostitution, and the black market have reduced the nation to a state of decadence unparalleled in history."

It called on all Catholics "to collaborate in all efforts, whatever their origin, to carry out a revolution intended to clean up society and build a new, just, free society." This was a notable declaration because Catholics had, in the past, been among Thieu's most loyal supporters.

Two months later the People's Anti-Corruption Movement held a demonstration in Hue at which their chief spokesman, Father Tran Huu Thanh, read what he called "Public Indictment No. 1," consisting of charges against Thieu and his family.

Among the allegations were these:

The president had taken advantage of his position to acquire several houses and large pieces of land.

Thieu and Prime Minister General Tran Thien Khiem were involved in heroin traffic.

An artificial rice shortage had been created in central Vietnam by speculators including Mme. Ngo Thi Huyet, aunt of the president and mother of Hoang Duc Nha, his minister of information.

Thieu had protected Nguyen Xuan Nguyen, president of the Hai Long company, over fertilizer deals. (Nguyen's name was widely linked with the fertilizer scandal but it did not figure in the inquiry report.)

A People's Hospital founded by Mme. Thieu had been financed by the sale of smuggled goods and poor people had been refused admission to it.

The Catholics' demonstration was broken up by police with tear gas and clubs and, when three Saigon newspapers published the text of the Public Indictment nearly two weeks later, the police confiscated the copies. One editor was charged with libeling Thieu.

The president made his reply in a two-hour broadcast in which he was incoherent at times. He swore that he had never taken a bribe, promised that if his relatives had broken the law they would be punished, and said he had ordered a drive against corruption in the army and civil service.

He began the drive—in fact, he had already acted—by dismissing two divisional commanders, Generals Lai Van Tu and Tran Quoc Lich, for selling rice to the enemy. In the days that followed he accepted the resignations of four members of his cabinet including Nguyen Duc Cuong, the minister of trade, whose dismissal had been called for by the fertilizer inquiry. The Defense Ministry announced the names of 377 colonels and majors to be dismissed for "corruption and dishonest activities." Then Thieu removed three of the four current corps commanders, General Nguyen Van Toan of the Second, General Pham Quoc Thuan of the Third, and General Nguyen Vinh Nghi of the Fourth.

Father Thanh intensified his campaign. He and a group of opposition leaders demanded the prosecution of Mme. Thieu, accusing her of land speculation. They also charged that the president and Mme. Thieu had received $7 million from the United States at the end of 1972 for agreeing to the Paris accord.

Thanh went on to call for Thieu's trial for treason, accusing him of having "abused the anti-Communist cause to appropriate power for himself and to serve the interests of his own family and group." This was his Public Indictment No. 2.

Nine newspapers published this, but all copies were seized by the police, five newspapers were suppressed, and eighteen journalists were arrested.

Later Father Thanh became one of my staunchest supporters in the National Salvation Committee, but both his Anti-Corruption Movement and the National Salvation Committee were overrun by the Communist military machine and one can only speculate about what might have been achieved.

Even in the final throes of the war, in April 1975, there were fresh allegations of corruption. *The Washington Post* alleged that military aid amounting to more than $200 million had been lost or squandered by the Thieu government, a large amount of it being stolen by officials of the Saigon government and sold to the enemy.

Among losses said to have been listed in secret reports prepared by the United States General Accounting Office, the financial watchdog for Congress, were 143 vessels, including patrol boats and landing craft that disappeared from the South Vietnamese Navy. Embassy sources were quoted as saying that General Nguyen Vinh Nghi, former commander of South Vietnamese forces in the Mekong Delta, had pilfered 8,000 radios and 24,000 small arms from U.S. equipment, selling most of them to the Viet Cong.

How far Thieu personally was guilty, as charged by Father Thanh, I cannot say, though I know that Mme. Thieu sported an ostentatious diamond and that the president amassed a fortune in France and Switzerland. I was told that he sought to arrange for an American airliner to fly seventeen tons of his possessions out of Saigon. I do not know whether he succeeded in this, but when he left with General Khiem on April 26 for Taiwan, where his brother was South Vietnam's ambassador, it was said he took with him five suitcases stuffed with dollars.

Perhaps all presidents of unstable countries develop a fixation about providing for themselves in the event of loss of office. When I attended the Manila conference with the heads of government of America, Australia, New Zealand, Thailand, and South Korea in 1966, our host, President Marcos of the Philippines, took me aside to offer me what he obviously felt was wise counsel to a young man. "You have to think about your future, about the danger of a coup," he said. "Just supposing something happens, take my advice. I always have two suitcases by my bedside."

I never acquired one suitcase, let alone two.

Certainly, corruption was rife in Vietnam, but what other country can say it is free from corruption? It is a question of degree, really. I remember when visiting Williamsburg on my American tour in 1970, I spoke to a deputation of youngsters who were protesting against the Vietnam war. After I had explained to them in the hotel lobby how I felt, I asked them if they had anything more to say. One youngster held up his hand and cried, "We are against the corruption in your country."

"So am I," I retorted. "What you say is true. We do have corruption. But what about your society? You are supposed to be the most organized, the most advanced country in the world today. Are you fully satisfied with your system? Are you sure there is no corruption in America?"

There was no reply. I added, "Maybe we do have a little

more corruption than you because we are not such a well-organized society, and also remember we have been at war for twenty-four years. But corruption is only a question of degree. Do you really think you have any right to criticize Vietnamese corruption unless you are sure that you have none in your own country?"

Only once, to my knowledge, was I the subject of allegations myself. That was when, in 1973, I decided to start a large commune with a group of sixty officers in virgin jungle in the Highlands. In those days it was possible to buy undeveloped land for 500 piastres (about $5) a hectare, and to borrow money from the Vietnam National Development Bank to purchase machinery to clear the land and start farming.

There was only one snag. This cheap land was available only to civilians. I was in a curious position. I was still in the air force, yet, in a way, I was a civilian because I had no authority. However, since I *did* have rank, legally the land was denied me. So I bought 200 hectares in the Khanh Duong district, about 200 miles north of Saigon, in my wife's name. This led to a press campaign that my wife was speculating in land. This was nonsense because all we were trying to do was to supplement my meager pay and develop new land, and President Thieu had done everything in his power to help. It was with his blessing that we obtained the cooperation of the local authorities and were able to get loans for machinery and building material from the bank. (Unfortunately, I still owe the bank 19 million piastres!)

However, I must confess that I did yield to temptation once, when I was prime minister. General Westmoreland came to see me to beg some ground on which to build a military headquarters. I had already provided some ground near my airfield to house Vietnamese officers, who had built a delightful community for themselves, and I suggested a stretch of open ground near that.

Westmoreland and I visited it together and then drove back to the airfield. Just outside the perimeter was a soccer field. "That's about the size of place I want," said Westmoreland, "and that would be much handier, being so close to the base."

I told him it was impossible. "We couldn't take the boys' field away from them."

Nothing more was said at the time, but a few days later a junior officer from the American staff brought me some reading matter on the new American HU 1B helicopter, a magnificent machine that could carry fourteen passengers for two hours or more. I was fascinated, for I was still flying an old French helicopter at the time.

When Westmoreland and I next dined together he asked, "How did you like the specifications of the new chopper?" I told him that it looked like the best helicopter in the world. Coffee was served, then he said casually: "About building the headquarters. Is it quite impossible to have that field?"

I said I did not see how it could be done.

"Well," said Westmoreland, "I'll tell you what I'll do. If you let me have the field, I'll give you two new helicopters."

Every man has his price and mine was a flying machine.

10

AID:

Knots in the strings

When you are a small country, fighting for your existence, and you are on the receiving end of foreign aid, there is little you can do except utter a grateful "Thank you." No one realizes more than I that a huge nation like the United States cannot just dole out vast sums of money without some sort of check on what happens to it. And yet, if strings are attached to foreign aid, and if the knots on those strings are tied too tightly, there is a real danger that both donor and receiver lose out in the end.

This has nothing to do with the gratitude of the Vietnamese for the unstinted generosity of the American aid program over the years, and it may seem ill-mannered to cavil now. But I am not doing that. I am putting on record views based on experience that I have voiced whenever possible.

Over the years I had expressed my fears and doubts to American leaders, but never more strongly than in 1970 during my semi-private visit to the United States, when I traveled around the country in the president's Boeing 707.

Almost as soon as I arrived, I went for a White House working breakfast at 7:30 A.M. with President Nixon. Kissinger and other officials were present and I steered the talk around to American aid, the way it was being administered, and even more important, the way in which it was being tied with red tape.

"The trouble is," I told the president, "the strings attached to your aid program so often lead to more and more corruption in Vietnam." Nixon was sitting opposite me, and I could see

117

that I was perhaps talking a little too bluntly, but I was determined to give the president a few examples.

The strings I had in mind were many and tangled. For example, we received a great deal of milk from the United States that we needed badly. This milk had to be paid for from the dollars we received in aid, but that milk turned sour in two ways.

First, the milk originated not from the West Coast of America but from the East Coast because the United States government had a contract there. This increased the freight charges enormously. Worse, I found that we could have bought milk of similar quality in Singapore at almost half the American price. I appreciated that most money granted in aid must be spent in the country of origin; this is implicit in such deals. But when a country is fighting for its life there must be exceptions. Even if the United States government refused to allow us to spend our dollars in Singapore, we could have bought milk more cheaply on the West Coast of America, but I had the feeling that someone had been lobbying Congress and there was no way around the deal.

Another example of the problems concerned the mundane but essential item of fertilizers. It was a sore point that stretched back to the time when I was prime minister in 1966. One of my main objectives had been to improve the economic situation in Vietnam. To do this we had to increase agricultural production, and we were buying $2 million worth of fertilizer a year from our allies. With the lower labor rates in Vietnam, to say nothing of the saving on freight charges, we could have produced fertilizer more cheaply. Obviously we could not afford to build a factory ourselves, but about this time the British offered to build one for us.

"British interests have agreed to finance the construction of the factory," the British ambassador told me, "it won't cost you a penny and we will run it for you until you want us to hand it over." Then came the reason for the visit. Wryly the ambassador added, "I've come to you personally, Prime Minister, because I know *you* need the fertilizer and *we* would like to build the factory, but my commercial attachés can't get anywhere with your government when they try to obtain the necessary planning permission."

It seemed to me a wonderful opportunity but, as I told President Nixon, though I tried, I could not buck American red tape. There was a contract for fertilizers and, even if we could produce our own at half the price, the Americans adamantly said "No." It took me three years to persuade the Americans even to consider allowing us to build a plant, and then only because finally I went to Ambassador Lodge. He agreed that it was the right thing to do and cabled Washington, or I presume he did, and everyone seemed to agree that this was in the best interests of Vietnam. But that fertilizer factory was never built, and after 1973, when I was a private citizen hacking out a farm from jungle, I had to buy all my fertilizer on the black market.

If the Americans had been able to agree with me in 1966, the factory could have been in production by 1968 when the government started to implement its plan for agricultural development.

I appreciate that with the U.S. Congress having to vote appropriations there must be some restrictions, if only to safeguard the ultimate destination of the cash involved. But sometimes the restrictions can be too severe. When the French gave us freedom—or rather when the Vietnamese beat them, and they had to leave—the French gave us aid. They had a phrase that I remember: "We give you the money with an elastic band around it." Sometimes I wonder if the American elastic band was not too tight.

President Nixon listened patiently to my tales of woe, and finally promised me, "Mr. Vice President, I'll send a new team of economists to Vietnam and if they can see anything that we can change, we'll do it right away."

Nothing changed materially. -

People are not always aware of the way in which aid money is handled, and I am the first to admit that there were problems. Under the Commercial Import Program, we bought products like milk and fertilizers through a system of grants.

Vietnamese importers ordered the goods we required (with the blessing of the government) and the United States paid the American sellers directly in dollars. The Vietnamese importers, who were normal commercial firms, paid for the goods in piastres. These piastres were deposited in a counterpart fund which the United States government then made available to the South Vietnamese government to pay the armed forces and the civil service. About 80 percent of this money was used on defense expenditure.

By the time I raised the matter with the president the Americans had been pouring money into Vietnam for two decades. The first aid was military and was delivered to the French, thanks to the Mutual Defense Assistance Act of 1949, under which the United States provided military help to the newly formed North Atlantic Treaty Organization, to Greece and Turkey, Iran, Korea, the Philippines, and Nationalist China. France received some $20 million in the first year and, though it was intended to strengthen NATO, the French, anxious to restore their colonial supremacy, craftily diverted some of the equipment to Indochina.

The following year Secretary of State Dean Acheson announced that American aid would be given to the French for direct use against the Vietminh, and the first arms were flown to Saigon in July 1950. The following month, President Truman's Military Assistance Advisory Group arrived to handle distribution to the French of bombers, tanks, and ammunition —all intended to kill Vietnamese.

Between then and the defeat of the French in 1954 the Americans sent military equipment worth $2.6 billion and met some 80 percent of the costs of the vain French struggle to retain their mastery of our country. How ironical that the Americans backed a loser, even then.

During the same period the Bao Dai government was given more than $100 million in direct military, economic, and technical aid. The Americans recognized that it was not enough to win the war against Communism with bullets; Indochina had to be made economically stable and prosperous if Communist ideology was not to spread. So their aid program dealt with the

South Vietnamese President Ngo Dinh Diem speaks at a conference circa 1957. *(Getty Images)*

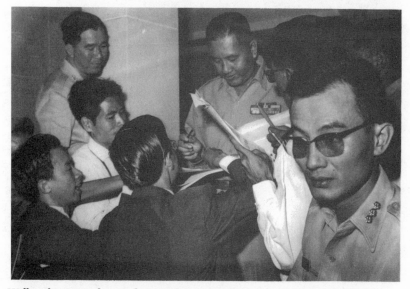

Well-wishers crowd around General Duong Van Minh following the 1963 coup. *(The Vietnam Archive, Texas Tech University)*

SEATO nations leaders stand for a group portrait at the Manila Conference in 1966. L-R: Nguyen Cao Ky; Prime Minister Harold Holt (Australia); President Park Chung Hee (Korea); President Ferdinand Marcos (Philippines); Prime Minister Keith Holyoake (New Zealand); Lt. General Nguyen Van Thieu (South Vietnam); Prime Minister Thanom Kittakachorn (Thailand); President Lyndon Johnson (United States). *(LBJ Library Photo by Frank Wolfe)*

Buddhist monks demonstrate to demand fair treatment. (*The Vietnam Archive, Texas Tech University*)

Captured Viet Cong are paraded during the Communist Tet offensive in Quang Ngai, along with a black marketer (right). (*The Vietnam Archive, Texas Tech University*)

An American soldier, Lt. Col. John Hemphill, displays a captured woven portrait, or "inspirational" banner, of Ho Chi Minh, president of North Vietnam. (*The Vietnam Archive, Texas Tech University*)

South Vietnamese Premier General Nguyen Khanh. (*Hulton/Archive by Getty Images*)

(L-R) Secretary of State Robert McNamara, Prime Minister Nguyen Cao Ky, President Lyndon Johnson, and Lt. General Nguyen Van Thieu speak at the Honolulu Conference in 1966. *(LBJ Library Photo by Yoichi Okamoto)*

President Thieu stands in front of a world map at the White House. *(LBJ Library Photo by Yoichi Okamoto)*

Vietnamese rangers on an operation to rout the Viet Cong between Binh Tien Bridge and Binh Tay alcohol distillery in Cholon, following attacks on Saigon and nearby areas during the Tet holiday period in 1968. (*The Vietnam Archive, Texas Tech University*)

Descending the steps of Saigon's Independence Palace prior to their appearance before the press are Presidents Thieu and Nixon. Behind them, from right, are United States Ambassador to Vietnam Ellsworth Bunker, Vice President Nguyen Cao Ky, and Henry Kissinger, special advisor to President Nixon. President Nixon made an unannounced five-hour visit to South Vietnam on July 30, 1969. *(The Vietnam Archive, Texas Tech University)*

Corpses lie on the pavement while soldiers question a prisoner in Vietnam. (*Hulton/Archive by Getty Images*)

Vietnamese at village level. They built roads and irrigation systems, they distributed clothing and medicine, they extended social welfare.

Yet the dreams failed. The French saw the United States creating a new nation and threatening French interests, while the average Vietnamese found it difficult to understand why the Americans should give them roads, food, drugs to make life easier, and at the same time give the French guns and bombs to kill them.

The Americans were convinced that the French would win the war by 1954. Instead there came Dien Bien Phu and the defeat of the French, but America continued to aid Vietnam under the umbrella of the South East Asia Treaty Organization, which it hoped would protect it from accusations of colonialist intervention. At first United States aid was used principally to pay the costs of the Vietnamese Army and to assist in the re-settlement of refugees.

President Eisenhower sent General J. Lawton Collins to Vietnam as his personal envoy to supervise the start of a military training program while, at the same time, America provided funds for a land reform program. This was to resettle refugees from the North and land-seeking peasants in former swamp, forest, and mountain areas of central Vietnam. These communities were given names like "agrovilles" and even "prosperity centers" but the people tended to drift away.

By 1956 the United States was paying the Diem regime an average of $270 million a year, more aid per head of the population than it spent on any other country in the world except Laos and Korea. (Its other commitments among under-developed countries included the Philippines, India, and Taiwan.)

In the first five years of the Diem regime a quarter of a billion dollars was provided, which covered the whole of the South Vietnamese armed forces and 80 percent of all other government expenditure. America paid the annual trade deficit of $178 million; it subsidized Diem completely. And it considered the money well spent.

There were many of us who did *not* think the money well

spent, as we watched the wicked antics of Diem's brother Nhu and his wife, and in a way that was another string attached to aid. The Americans believed in Diem and—until the veil was torn from their eyes—supported him in power, despite the growing restiveness among the young and ardent patriots who wanted a tougher government. It was not difficult for America to promote the image they required because there were few reporters in Saigon at this time and most of the information available to Americans came from government handouts, which extolled not only Diem's non-existent program but his deeply religious background, cemented by two years in America before his return to power. So the aid flowed in—everything from pigs to plastic limbs, from barbed wire to prefabricated buildings, from chicken feed to air conditioners. I shudder to think how much of a rake-off Nhu got on every shipment. For that is yet another tragic aspect of aid offered with an open, generous heart, but offered to the wrong people—much of it is wasted when it goes to the wrong man, an aloof, remote president in the hands of crooks.

And too, as I told President Nixon, it has to be the *right* kind of aid. It is no use sending Switzerland a fleet of battleships, or the people of Christmas Island a fleet of bombers. Though we were grateful to President Johnson for the magnificent promises he made in his 1965 speech at Johns Hopkins University, some of us felt first things should be first.

Johnson said he would ask Congress to endorse a billion-dollar American investment program in the South East Asia area that would include the development of the Mekong River Valley "on a scale to dwarf even our own Tennessee Valley Authority."

Hanoi's reaction was predictable: the offer was a bribe to bring the war to an end. Our reaction in South Vietnam was simple: let's win the war first, then make far-reaching social and economic plans.

Yet how *dare* a poor nation refuse such a magnificent gesture? When you are struggling for your very existence, no one can look any gift horse in the mouth. Yet Johnson's speech pinpoints another aid problem: *who* should choose? Is it necessarily best for the ally and friend to decide what is best for the poor relation? It may be pleasant to receive a tie from your wife for Christmas, but you may hate it. Would it not be wiser if your wife asked you to go shopping with her? All too often we found ourselves burdened with extraordinary quantities of unwanted goods, as happened in the village of Tuylon, west of Danang. One fine morning an American helicopter landed near the paddy fields, and out tumbled a squad of United States Marines, led by a sergeant called Melvin Murrell.

They had not come to fight, but as part of the pacification program—in other words, to win the hearts and minds of the population of Tuylon. Whether they did so is open to question, though they certainly arrived armed with gifts and goodwill. The most astonishing gift of all consisted of 7,000 toothbrushes —the large number due to some error in accounting back at base. The village chief was staggered when he was presented with four portable lavatories. Each one had a flushing device operated by batteries. The women of the village were equally mystified when Sergeant Murrell presented them with cartons. How eagerly they must have torn the tops open! Each carton contained, of all things, "Uncle Ben's" rice. Only the children's hearts and minds were easily won over without any of them having to think, for even the rich rice fields of Tuylon could not grow Hershey bars.

Many unfortunate effects and side effects were not always the fault of the Americans. They were most helpful to me when we developed "New Life Hamlets" in 1967. These were villages in which the inhabitants were expected to make a major share of the decisions. We would gather the villagers together and it would be up to them to decide whether they wanted money spent on a well or on grain or whatever. The Americans never tried to impose their way of life on the country as, perhaps, they tended to do in the city. But, of course, as in the military area, it is impossible for enthusiasts of any nation to hand out huge sums of money and advice without thinking in terms of their own life-styles; and the presence of American advisers tended to make many of the villages utterly dependent on them, which was exactly the opposite of what the Americans intended, and which had disastrous effects when the Americans pulled out.

Time after time I begged American advisers to keep more in the background, in the same way as the Chinese and Russians remained in the background. I wanted the villagers to feel that, even if the aid did come from the United States, the *idea* was ours, Vietnamese. As indeed it often was. I initiated the New Life Hamlets when I created the Revolutionary Development Committee after becoming prime minister, and this to me was part of my plan for winning the hearts and minds of the people, of trying to show the villagers that we, with our ideas, could offer them a better way of life than Communism. It did not work. Most people in rural areas who benefited were firmly convinced that they were living in "American villages." Many of the older generation, whose life revolved around the village and family, seemed to think they had merely exchanged their French masters for new ones; while more than one youngster nurtured on skillful anti-American propaganda turned his thoughts to the North where, knowing nothing of the roles of Russia and China, he visualized a picture of life that might be hard and dangerous, but where (so he believed) men were "free" of outside interference.

I know it sounds ungrateful to criticize a nation that has, since 1950, spent $1.5 billion on military assistance to Vietnam and $5 billion in aid grants and credits, but ingratitude has nothing to do with it. America is the richest and most powerful nation on earth, and as the Third World emerges—even if our country is in darkness—America's role will become ever greater in shaping the destinies of these nations. So this is really a plea, learned from bitter experience, for more cooperation in aid, more flexibility between a country throwing off the shackles of the past and a mighty nation which believes above all in freedom, and is prepared, as it always has been, to back up its beliefs with a check. Let it, on occasion, be an open check.

11

TRAINING AN ARMY:

A question of advise and consent

Despite the enthusiasm and goodwill, despite the good intentions, the American advisory program was a lamentable disaster that contributed largely to the eventual debacle in Vietnam. It was worse: it was a gigantic con trick foisted on American public opinion. Not so much by those in the field as by those who never walked the field of battle, but strode the corridors of power in Washington, those to whom the Vietnam war started as a kind of theoretical dream of how to combat the spread of Communism, but gradually twisted and writhed into a hellish nightmare.

Many factors contributed to the problems facing U.S. military advisers—character differences, language, even superstition—but behind the local problems loomed one more sinister than all the rest. As America became more deeply involved, as the American death toll mounted, as American public opinion became more outraged, United States presidents became so fearful that their policies would rebound on them that none who worked closely with them dared to tell the truth.

Instead they settled for reassurance. One after another they reassured their president that the Vietnamese Army was in fine shape, not to worry about the American presence, for each month of advisory training was a month nearer the date when the Vietnamese Army could stand alone and win.

Year after year—in power and out—I watched as the wishful thinking grew into a cloud of hopeless exaggeration, if not downright lies, until finally it hung, like the mushroom of an A-bomb, across the land.

Let me say that no one can blame the dedicated American officers who tried to train us. They came from the cream of the United States Army, they were convinced they could do the job assigned to them. They were not afraid to venture out of their air-conditioned cocoons to the wet, embracing heat of a Vietnamese camp. But it was never possible to transform overnight—using the word *overnight* in terms of history—an Oriental army into a Western fighting force. The rule book, of course, said that it *was* possible. It had said so when the American advisory teams succeeded in Greece in 1949, and later in Korea—two countries in which conditions of fighting and training were totally different.

Few would admit that the rule book was wrong, though I knew personally of two fine American officers who resigned because they were so outraged by the false reports sent to Washington. The tragedy lay in the fact that nobody could persuade the powers-that-be to change the rules. If America could chalk up successes in Greece and Korea what was to stop them from registering another success in Vietnam? After all, as I heard one American veteran of Korea say without a trace of sarcasm, "What the hell's the difference between Vietnam and Korea anyway?" To him both were wet and hot, both offered the same kind of pretty, available girls, and he even ate the same kind of food in Vietnam that he had eaten in Korea, or for that matter in his transit camp back home.

The major problem—that of telling the truth—started with smaller problems, such as the fundamental differences in character: impatience versus patience. The American is by nature ebullient. His attitude when faced with any problem is, "Come on! Let's get it over with." In a highly psychological relationship between two men of totally different races, this uninhibited American enthusiasm actually bewildered his Vietnamese counterpart, whose nature was cautious and patient, not only by character but because his forebears had instinctively reacted that way to their colonial masters, the French. Sometimes it was hard for a young Vietnamese officer to realize that the Americans were friends, not new overlords.

This was no reflection on the Americans, who persisted with

admirable restraint, and were convinced they could finally teach the Vietnamese all their know-how, and Westernize them.

The advisers were hand-picked and it broke my heart to see them arrive in Vietnam, rosy-cheeked, bubbling with enthusiasm, and then—if they happened to be working in my area— to watch the frustration slowly setting in.

Language, of course, was always an insurmountable barrier, even if, as happened later, the American adviser had a smattering of Vietnamese. Both sides, to say nothing of the luckless interpreter, became hopelessly bogged down when trying to explain the technicalities of how to fight jungle warfare.

I remember once listening unseen in the next room to an interpreter—who spoke more than passable English—as he paid grave attention to the American officer explaining different methods of laying an ambush. As the interpreter translated, I realized that he had missed the sense of the argument. The words were more or less the same, but the emphasis was different. Imagine the problems both sides faced when explaining how to dismantle a machine gun!

Sometimes the two sides could never get together because of entirely different approaches. On one occasion I was present when an adviser was explaining the values of tear gas to clear an enemy stronghold. The young but keen Vietnamese officer looked doubtful, and the equally young American asked what the problem was.

"It's a wonderful idea," said the Vietnamese, "but it's the wrong time of year."

"It's never the wrong time of year for killing Commies!" said the American cheerfully.

The Vietnamese agreed, but pointed out that this was a season of strong winds and if the wind blew the gas away the attack would have failed.

"So what?" asked the American. "We've got plenty of gas; we just start over the next day."

"But if the wind blows the gas away," persisted the Vietnamese, "everyone in the area will believe that God is on the side of the Communists."

The American was admirable in the way he kept his patience in the face of such obvious nonsense. But was it nonsense? Not to the superstitious Vietnamese, who can read a sign from the Almighty in anything from a teacup to a sudden thunderstorm that douses an American napalm raid—thus proving to most Vietnamese that the Americans were wrong to bomb that particular area; otherwise, why did the Gods arrange the storm?

Up against this kind of attitude, in conjunction with the legacy of a French-trained colonial army, plus the need to keep a worried president happy, and the fact that they had to make monthly progress reports, most American advisers did the only thing possible in the circumstances: they tended to ignore "difficult" Vietnamese officers and single out for promotion the lazy ones who quickly realized that the simplest course was to sit back and agree with everything, as their fathers had politely pretended to agree with everything the French had told them. Those who had learned the basic arts of counterinsurgency and guerrilla warfare with the Vietminh when they were fighting the French, tended to be discarded. For now the war was being run on Western lines.

As one American said to me, "Sure, Uncle Ho beat the French, but the Communists can never beat us—provided you remember that we turn out better boys at West Point than the French ever did in their military academy, St Cyr."

So the American advisers had to deceive themselves, and this resulted in the supreme irony of all: the best Vietnamese were rarely in line for promotion, the yes-men went right to the top. It led to a fundamental weakness in the Vietnamese Army that showed up in those last frightful weeks. The debacle, then, can be traced right back to the fact that in order to reassure a president over 6,000 miles away, the American advisers tended to pick the wrong men to lead our army; the Vietnamese soldiers in turn became disheartened, their morale fell to zero as they realized the kind of officers who led them. It is sad but true: the bright young Vietnamese interfered with the "pattern" of American training. He posed awkward questions to which there were no answers in the American rule book.

To this state of affairs can be added the simple human factor that any officer's career in any army in any part of the world depends on results, on his ability, so the American adviser tended to exaggerate his achievements in his regular reports, with the result that the men he had picked out gained even more promotion.

The White House was happy though ignorant. The job of the president's men in Washington was to prove that America was training an elite officer corps in Vietnam ready to take over and win the war. In fact the Americans were training an army to become more and more dependent on America.

It was also difficult to buck the American rule book in other ways, when it came to training troops.

Our great problem was time—lack of time to train Vietnamese troops as one would train them in peacetime. But if the American rule book said that one hundred rookies needed barracks with twenty-five rooms, then the training didn't start until the rooms had been found. When I suggested the rookies could sleep in tents or, if necessary, on the beach, out came the regulation books.

I took up the point with Melvin Laird, Secretary of Defense, at the Pentagon, when I visited Washington, suggesting one simple solution: "Why not cut the period of training from six months to three months? Don't you think it is possible in time of war?"

Laird agreed, "You're right; I know it can be done because we did it in World War II."

"Well," I asked, "why not do it in Vietnam now?"

There was no answer really except, of course, that nobody in Vietnam had bothered to suggest it to Laird. Once we talked it over man to man, this procedure was implemented immediately.

The first steps to build a South Vietnamese army to halt the march of Communism had been taken in 1954, when Diem, the new prime minister, wanted the French out rapidly. America begged to be allowed to train South Vietnam's forces, and General Collins was sent to arrange the details with the French and Vietnamese.

An American mission, he announced, would soon "take charge of instructing the Vietnam Army in accordance with special American methods which have proved effective in Korea, Greece, and Turkey. The mission will work under the supervision of General Paul Ely (the French commissioner). The aim will be, however, to build a completely autonomous Vietnam Army."

In February 1955 America's Military Assistance Advisory Group, which had been established in Saigon since 1950, took over the training, and the French prepared to withdraw. The MAAG, under General Sam Williams, disbanded the small French-trained forces, replacing them with seven regular divisions armed with American weapons. Then they added marines, Rangers, airborne battalions, a navy, and an air force, creating a miniature version of the United States armed forces. Thousands of officers were sent to Fort Bragg and other camps in the United States for training.

At the same time they recruited a civil guard for regional defense (Regional Forces) and a self-defense corps to protect villages (the Popular Forces). A chain of command was established from village chiefs to military province chiefs to four corps commanders to the government.

Here again, the advice was wrong. The plans had been based on practice in South Korea, but though it might have been sound there, it did not suit us. We were waging a different kind of war. The army, with all its component parts, was designed to meet a full-scale invasion from the North. Its task was to defend South Vietnam at the 17th parallel, in the comparatively narrow space between Laos and the sea. But the Viet Cong did not launch a frontal attack. They infiltrated men into South Vietnam by the mountain paths of Laos and the Army of the Republic of (South) Vietnam (ARVN) had to fight a guerrilla war inside our own country.

What happened is history—and a terrible tragedy. The Communist tactics made nonsense of our vast numerical superiority. Our strategy was defensive. The army trained by Americans had to be spread across the country. The Communists merely looked around until they found a weak spot, then attacked.

Because these were "terrorist" attacks, the Americans even ruled at first that they were the concern of the police (as they often had been in Malaya). But our National Police Force was a Cinderella service, staffed by men over military age, and mostly on a daily pay basis. I met many brave men among them, but I never met any suitably trained and equipped to take on the Viet Cong. The Regional Forces were confined to their own provinces and they too were poorly paid and often armed with obsolete weapons.

The picture was not all black. Our marines and Special Forces, trained largely by the Americans, became the equal of any in the world, but here again there were problems. The advice in *training* was excellent; but the advice in *employing* this crack body of men was not always good. The Special Forces, in their distinctive green berets, were trained to search and destroy, living in the jungle for weeks on end if necessary. That was their role in the early days when I and my colleagues in the air force dropped them by parachute.

But gradually their role was diminished. Because they were so expert they were dispersed and attached to various army units where they were used, not for killing the enemy, but for making reconnaissance forays before an attack. This meant that they could not kill; they had to go into the jungle stealthily and return with information undetected. We needed the information but it was a waste of a crack force to use them like this. A few months before the end, I proposed that they be reorganized into one fighting division, but my proposal came to nothing.

When a war is spread over years, great changes must occur in the roles of the fighting forces, and after the faults in training, which gave us many poor senior officers, came an incident that cast grave doubts in American minds on the efficiency of the Vietnamese troops they had trained.

On January 2, 1963, a Communist force surrounded an ARVN group many times its size at Ap Bac in the Mekong Delta, fifty miles from Saigon. The Communists shot down five American helicopters and damaged nine, killing three Americans and bringing American casualties in the war to thirty. The ARVN let the Communists escape and, though General Paul Harkins claimed a victory, and though President Kennedy declared in his State of the Union message on January 14, "The spearhead of aggression has been blunted in Vietnam," recriminations and inquiries followed.

In itself this incident might have been forgotten, but in less than a year came the naval action in the Gulf of Tonkin when American ships were attacked by North Vietnamese gunboats in August—on the day before I, as the youngest of the Young Turks, played a major role in the reorganization of the armed forces. In the Tonkin incident no Vietnamese were involved, but perhaps because of American lack of confidence after Ap Bac, the Tonkin incident brought about a fundamental change in the roles of the American and Vietnamese troops. The Americans flew in fifty jets to provide fire power; they brought in American marines and South Korean troops. Soon they were committed to fighting, rather than advising and training. The Americans took on the attacking role that the ARVN had never been trained, nor equipped, to perform, as the war was carried to North Vietnam.

I hated to see our army denied the chance to attack, but there was nothing I could do about it, even as prime minister when, in 1967, I held discussions with McNamara and formalized a shift in the role of the ARVN.

McNamara was by then opposing any increase in the American war effort. He doubted if the war could be won in less than two years, so he wanted to enliven the program of pacification, to secure areas that we held. I did not expect enemy activity to decrease; indeed, I expected it to increase, so I agreed about the importance of pacification.

Together we clarified the respective roles of the South Vietnamese and American forces. As a result, between January and July 1967, I shifted all ARVN infantry divisions to pacification and gave additional power to General Nguyen Duc Thang, director of my Revolutionary Development program.

I saw this as part of a two-year schedule extending through

1967 and 1968, under which offensive operations would be carried out primarily by the Americans and third-country forces. By the end of two years I believed the enemy might be prepared to negotiate. The plan was sound, but it failed to achieve the hoped-for results.

12

HEARTS AND MINDS:

How the battle was lost

Alongside the military war, fought with bombs and bullets, we had to fight another war—one to convince our own people that South Vietnam offered a way of life superior to that of the Communists. It was a war for the hearts and minds of the people.

It was not, as some thought, a matter of simple materialism, a philosophy that started with filling bellies. Ambassador Ellsworth Bunker was hopelessly wrong when he told me on one occasion, "People are drifting toward Communism because they are poor. If you give the people everything they want—television sets, automobiles, and so on—none of them will go over to Communism."

Poor Bunker! He was trying to impose American standards of life on people he did not understand, people who basically had no desire for the so-called good things of the American way of life.

Like so many well-meaning Americans, Bunker, when he came to Vietnam, was unable to grasp the fact that he had made an excursion into a culture as different from America's as an African Negro's is different from that of an Eskimo. No man could hope to span the differences in American and Vietnamese culture and heritage in the short time of his appointment in our land. How could I explain to Bunker's Western mind, for example, that while an American would be lost without a future to conquer, a Vietnamese is lost without the refuge of the past.

"Material goods are not the answer," I replied. "It's much

more important to win the hearts and minds of the people than to give them TV sets."

Bunker shook his head disbelievingly, and I felt, watching him, that he was wondering how this young upstart dared to utter such nonsense. But then Bunker no doubt believed in Napoleon's dictum that an army marches on its stomach, and saw no reason why civilians should be any different. But they were.

Among my first priorities when I became prime minister was to introduce some form of social revolution, a term I later amended to "social justice." My aims, my hopes, were very simple: I wanted my people to get a proper reward for their efforts. I wanted a man working eight hours a day to receive twice as much as a man working four hours a day. It takes very little to make the Vietnamese happy. Our needs are simple because we are Asians; we are influenced by the sayings of Confucius. We are not interested in material gain like Westerners; commercial success does not attract us as it does Americans, so we can be happy with little. On the other hand, we do not like to feel exploited, and there lay the root of our problem.

For above all else, the Communist cadres, infiltrating from the North, exploited our corruption and black marketeering as they tried to win over puzzled (yet at heart loyal) peasants to the cause of Ho Chi Minh. They were diabolically clever, for they made no spectacular promises; they held out no bribes. Like Churchill, they offered nothing but blood, sweat, toil, and tears, but they were able to build up the image of a simple, Spartan leader as great in his way as Churchill, and contrast it with our squabbling, corrupt politicians, as squalid in their way as the French politicians in 1940 who bickered among themselves while the Germans streamed across their land.

Yet we had one ace in our hand, if only we could play the hand properly, an ace that did not even exist in the Communist deck of cards. It was freedom, the world's most precious —yet most elusive—treasure. The freedoms that Roosevelt had preached, not only the freedom from fear and want, but the freedom for us to choose our leaders, and the freedom to boot them out if they proved unworthy of the trust reposed in them.

I felt we had to start at the top—and at the bottom. We needed to establish free elections at all levels—in the village tribunal as well as the presidential palace. We needed to introduce fair systems of compensation, provisions for social welfare—all things that are taken for granted in the West.

We achieved more than we were given credit for, though all our efforts were made against a backdrop of a bitter fight for survival. The draft continued in Vietnam until virtually the end, and at the height of the fighting every family in the country had one member, if not two or three, in uniform.

But if we held an ace, we also held a deuce. For while I was preaching the need for freedom, I was not always free myself. True, we were not puppets, yet we never achieved the standing or appearance of an independent, self-governing country. The Americans criticized us for not having a highly developed system of government, but how could we have that when every Vietnamese in Saigon referred to the American ambassador as "the Governor General"?

The Americans did not seek this; they were not colonists, but South Vietnam had been a colony until the defeat of the French, and in many ways it remained virtually a colony, though without the restrictions imposed by the French. We still lacked our own identity.

We never produced a leader to unite the country with its many religious and political factions. The North had one in Ho Chi Minh; rightly or wrongly, the Communists believed in him and fought and died for him. He had a charisma that won many supporters even in the West and not all of them were Communists. Neither Diem, nor Thieu—both backed by the Americans—won the hearts of even the South Vietnamese.

The Americans controlled the fighting of the war. American aid financed the country; without it we could not survive. Americans selected or influenced the selection of our politicians and leaders, even at village level, and had a natural tendency to pick the most compliant rather than the most gifted. American culture—its films, television, and advertising—swamped our own.

Conscious of their dollar-bought superiority, the Americans

patronized us at all levels. GIs thoughtlessly but hurtfully referred to Vietnamese as Dinks and Gooks, Slants and Slopes. (Charlie, Chuck, and Claude were reserved for the Viet Cong.)

Their contemptuous attitude was typified by an announcer on the American Forces Radio in 1970: "For those of you staying on in 'Nam, here's a little advice regarding our Vietnamese friends. As you know, they're kind of jumpy now, so please remember the golden rule. Never pat a Vietnamese on the head. Stand on low ground when you talk to them. They kind of resent looking up to you. Okay?"

Certainly the Vietnamese resented being patted on the head. The battle for the hearts and minds of the people was more fundamental to success even than air power or fire power. Yet someone, presumably a GI, painted in white letters on an old warehouse by the river in Saigon the legend: "Just grab the Gooks by the balls and their hearts and minds will follow."

Faced with these problems, the peasants of Vietnam became some of the war's most tragic casualties. All they asked for was the right to extract a living from the soil, as their forebears had done. Instead, millions became refugees, driven from their homes by either the Communists or, alas, the Americans.

When the French left, the peasants were given a new deal. Until then, most fertile land had been owned by rapacious landlords who let it to tenants on a crop-sharing arrangement, by which the owner sometimes received up to 70 percent of the worker's income. To meet his ongoing expenses until his harvest was in, the farmer had to borrow from equally rapacious moneylenders, usually Chinese, at exorbitant rates of interest.

In 1956, when a million refugees fled from the North to a country that had become derelict during the French–Vietnam war, the Diem government restricted land ownership to 100 hectares (245 acres). Anyone with a bigger holding had to sell the surplus to the government, receiving 10 percent of its value in cash, the rest in bonds. Half a million acres were acquired from landlords and shared among more than 120,000 tenants. And 160,000 hectares of wasteland were reclaimed: dams were built and irrigation systems constructed.

At the same time Diem opened an Agricultural Credits Organization to advance money to peasants to buy seeds and stock, and encouraged cooperatives to share tractors and machinery. The tenants paid for their land and repaid the loans by surrendering 20 percent of their crops for a number of years.

All went well, until the Communists realized the dangers and carried the war to the villages. Ruthlessly they killed headmen, abducted officials. The government tried to stem the brutality by creating defensive villages. Thousands of peasants were settled behind moats, ramparts of mud, barbed wire, and bamboo hedges, from which they could go out to work their fields during the day and to which they could return at night. There was nothing new in the idea. Vietnamese had done it centuries earlier when threatened by Chinese bandits. More recently the idea had worked successfully as a defense against Communist guerrillas in Malaya in the fifties.

But the Vietnamese peasants hated it and the first experiment lasted only a matter of months. Vietnamese peasants revere their ancestors and the ground their ancestors trod; by moving they lost their sense of identity and continuity. Yet defensive villages were necessary or the Communists would overrun the peasant population. So the government created "strategic hamlets."

The Americans backed the idea wholeheartedly, and by April 1963 Secretary of State Dean Rusk was claiming that "Already approximately seven million Vietnamese live in over five thousand strategic hamlets. The program calls for completion of another three thousand by the end of this year."

The truth is that only a relatively small percentage of them were viable. Some were situated in locations where defense was impossible and the Communists overran them. Some existed only on paper. They were never built because the peasants found that they could not get the relocation allowances they were promised and had to find the funds for creating fortified villages themselves.

Somehow, I had to make the scheme work. When I became prime minister I revived it under the name of "New Life Hamlets." But Diem had replaced the original landlords with officials, while I decided to replace the officials with freely elected village chiefs.

The Americans were very helpful—in some ways too helpful, because my communities frequently became known as "American villages." It was inevitable, I suppose, when American troops moved in by helicopter exuding goodwill, and distributing bars of chocolate, portable battery-operated lavatories, toothbrushes, and the "Uncle Ben's" rice to a knot of wondering and silent men, women, and children who had never asked for anything more than to be left alone to grow their own rice. But this was something the American GI could not understand. He had been sent to a village and knew only that he had to give the villagers their "basic liberties," as outlined in the Pacification Program Handbook, so that he could report back, "The friendship of the villagers was secured and they are with us in this war."

But the "friendship" was as short-lived as the bar of chocolate. The villagers were not *enemies*, but once the helicopter had whirred away, the chocolate, the comics, the portable lavatories were valueless against infiltrating Communists who slaughtered everyone who defied them.

General Westmoreland decided that the only hope of containing Communist guerrilla forces was to have areas between New Life Hamlets which would be designated as free-fire zones after they had been cleared of Communists. Anything that moved in that area could be shot. "Until now the war has been characterized by a substantial majority of the population remaining neutral," Westmoreland warned. "In the past year we have seen an escalation to a higher level of intensity in the war. This will bring about a moment of decision for the peasant farmer. He will have to choose if he stays alive.

"Until now the peasant farmer has had three alternatives. He could stay put and follow his natural instinct to stay close to the land, living beside the graves of his ancestors. He could move into an area under government control, or he could join the VC. Now, if he stays put, there are additional dangers.

"The VC cannot patch up wounds. If the peasant becomes a refugee he does get shelter, food and security, job opportunities and is given a hope to possibly return to the land. The third alternative is life with the VC. The VC have not made good on their promises; they no longer secure areas. There are B52 bombings, the VC tax demands are increasing, they want more recruits at the point of a gun, forced labor to move supplies. The battle is being carried more and more to the enemy."

Fine words; but when I read the speech, I saw its true meaning instantly: the Americans had abandoned hope of winning the loyalty of the peasants. They had given in to the cadres of the NLF and Viet Cong. And this meant an awful truth: from now on, there were to be no neutrals. Those who did not enter defensive villages or other government-controlled areas would have to suffer the consequences. Villages that went over to the Communists could—and would—be obliterated.

That almost standard, heartbreaking by-product of war emerged again. I saw it for myself. I remember taking up my helicopter one day, and suddenly seeing below me along a red road, under a blazing sun, a long snake of human beings winding its way endlessly. From where to where? There seemed to be millions of refugees, their pitiful belongings, their pots and pans and chickens carried on old men's backs, or jammed into baby carriages, old carts, or wheelbarrows. The line stretched from horizon to horizon, with here and there figures, perhaps left to die, littering the roadside as the slow-moving, almost Biblical caravan trudged toward a new life. Near the cities shanty towns sprang up overnight, homes made from gasoline cans or packing cases, hideous replicas of the poor but decent homes that had been drenched by the poison of men or burned with the fire of men.

The Americans distributed aid generously, and tried to create job opportunities, but it was impossible to make them understand what was involved in transplanting Vietnamese from one zone to another. Leaving aside the important aspect of ancestor worship and the dream of a perpetual family life, a Vietnamese village is a small, private world. Behind the bamboo hedge, ringed by rice fields, is a self-supporting world that has existed virtually unchanged for decades.

It was pointless for the Americans to promise better prospects for those who moved; they did not want better prospects. If the average villager amassed wealth it had to come from the land and that meant he was achieving his wealth at the expense of his neighbor. The Americans might earnestly believe that making money was the finest pursuit on earth. It was hard to explain to them that a villager who suddenly became rich was not so much respected as pointed at in shame.

Brought up in the beliefs of Confucianism, which is totally different from Christianity, the Vietnamese were content until they made contact with the West. From the moment the French arrived they changed the way of life in Vietnam as profoundly as Captain Cook changed life in Tahiti, and ever since that moment the Vietnamese, even without realizing it, have been engaged in a struggle to withstand the change or at least to adapt to the changes as peacefully as possible.

This instinctive inner struggle to maintain a way of life continued throughout the war against Communism. It may not seem so to many of the GIs who found our women so sensuous and often so willing, yet I think many Americans realized the undercurrent of resistance to change, the vain hope of clinging to a way of life that no country in the world has ever bettered. Why otherwise did so many GIs fall in love, not only with our women, but with our country?

13

LIMITED WAR:

America's fatal flaws

War is a horrible and messy business, and there are only two ways to fight one: an all-out attack that will crush an enemy as Hitler crushed France in 1940, or a limited war. To most soldiers the philosophy of fighting a war with one hand tied behind your back is irksome. But there are two sides to the question. With H-bombs ready to be used at the press of a button, and the consequent possibility of the human race becoming extinct, a limited war at least gives man the chance of survival. The wars in the Middle East have proved that.

But if you are to wage a limited war, then you must fight it according to rules that will allow you to win. The American politicians chose to fight a limited war because they rightly feared that if they smashed their way into North Vietnam, it would bring in China and Russia and lead to a third world war. The theory behind this belief was sound. The way in which the Americans implemented the theory lost the war for South Vietnam.

The Russians and Chinese also chose to fight a limited war, because they too feared that if they participated directly in force they would become involved in a world war that they could never hope to win. But they implemented their philosophy correctly and they won the war. For that is the blunt truth: without any Russians or Chinese killing any Americans, the two power blocs fought each other, using pawns in Vietnam, and the United States was defeated.

The Americans made two fundamental errors, which I pointed out to their leaders time and again when I was in office: you can fight a limited war only with subtlety, not by employing a juggernaut. And if you want to win, you must keep out of the limelight.

Firstly, how did the "juggernaut" arrive in Vietnam? The strength of what had begun modestly in 1950 as the United States Military Assistance Advisory Group rose in 1960 from 327 to 900; in 1961 it reached 3,200 and in 1962, when it was upgraded to the United States Military Assistance Command, Vietnam, under General Paul Harkins, it reached 11,300.

In 1963 it totaled 16,500 and in 1964, under General William Westmoreland, it became 23,300. In 1965, when American forces were committed to a fully combatant role, it grew to 180,000; in 1966 it was 389,000; in 1967 it was 463,000; in 1968 it was 495,000; and in 1969 it reached a peak of 541,500.

Even without South Vietnamese and other forces, an army of half a million men is a massive one and the Americans had aircraft carriers, jet bombers, and all the most modern, sophisticated, and deadly weapons of war. And yet they could not win the war because that army was the wrong army for a limited war.

The phrase "limited war" recurred constantly. The "Rolling Thunder" bombing campaign against North Vietnam that President Johnson ordered in 1965 was a campaign of "continuous limited air attacks." The targets were always limited by the politicians thousands of miles away.

General Maxwell Taylor, testifying before the Senate Foreign Relations Committee in 1966, said the United States aim was "to wage limited war" in Vietnam. Defense Secretary Robert McNamara, testifying before the Senate Preparedness Subcommittee in 1967, said there was no reason to believe that North Vietnam could be bombed to the negotiating table, and argued against expansion of air warfare.

Many American military leaders did believe they could destroy all North Vietnam's major airfields and fuel supplies in the first three days of an all-out air onslaught, but the politicians always ruled that the risks and costs were too great.

Targets had to be approved individually and many important ones were disallowed. So the bombing dragged on, with periodic halts for political maneuvering. Inevitably the bombing escalated and costs rose. In 1965, the first year of the Rolling Thunder campaign, individual flights against North Vietnam totaled 55,000; the tonnage of bombs dropped was 33,000; the aircraft lost numbered 171; and the direct operational costs were $460 million. In 1966 the flights totaled 148,000; the bomb tonnage was 128,000; the aircraft lost numbered 318; and the costs were $1.2 billion. And much of the effect was wasted.

When I was vice president in 1968 the Rolling Thunder target list was still the subject of innumerable restrictions. It was revised twice a month for the Secretary of Defense by the Joint Chiefs of Staff. Restrictions were particularly severe if targets recommended by the Joint Chiefs of Staff for bombing were within a ten-mile "prohibited circle" around Hanoi or a four-mile circle around Haiphong. These recommendations had to be evaluated by the Defense Department's I.S.A. office and approved by the Defense Secretary, the State Department, and the White House before the targets could be bombed. War can never have been fought before under such inhibitions.

The constraints were obvious. I remember reading a report of a barbecue held near President Johnson's home in Texas at which he said, "I have had advice to load our planes with bombs and to drop them on certain areas that I think would enlarge the war and escalate the war and result in our committing a good many American boys to fighting a war that I think ought to be fought by the boys of Asia to help protect their own land."

And when General Westmoreland in 1967 asked Johnson for 200,000 more troops (to bring his forces to 617,616) the president retorted, "When we add divisions, can't the enemy add divisions? If so, where does it all end?"

Of course America was wary of extending the war to a point that might have brought it into open conflict with Russia or China; it was equally understandable that it had to gauge how far public opinion would permit it to go. America did not want to fight an all-out war. Yet an army of half a million, with an arsenal of advanced weaponry, is an army for total war, not a limited one. If I had been in complete command of the war with half a million Americans under my orders I would have fought for a quick victory, and for that there is only one way—an all-out war with no holds barred. If we had fought that way we could have won.

On the other hand, if it had to be a limited war, if America had to maintain an accommodation with Russia and China, then there was no need to send half a million men. Right from the start America should have adopted a long-term plan and a patient attitude and been prepared to accept a people's war that might have taken another ten years to win, without causing all the divisiveness back home in the United States.

That war would have required no great army, no tragic American casualty lists. All we would have needed was help in training our troops, in bringing about social reforms to counter Communist propaganda, and in finding and training true leaders for tomorrow's Vietnam.

The Americans believed that by bulldozing tactics they could win quickly, even though fighting a limited war. But the two do not go together, and in any case a limited war can never yield a quick victory. The Americans also believed that they could win the people's war, the battle for the hearts of the people, while waging the military one. And they could not. The philosophy and strategy were wrong from the start and all that happened followed like a chain reaction.

I told all this to General Westmoreland, the U.S. commander from 1964 to 1968. I was commander of the air force when we first met and one of the Young Turks and I had been urging publicly that it was time to give youth a greater say in the direction of the war. I had been critical of the over-fifties. (I was thirty-four at the time.)

Westmoreland came to see me about my campaign and I told him I thought we should retire all the older officers. Perhaps I was a little tactless in being so blunt since Westmoreland was fifty, but our first meeting left me with the impression that we would never achieve a great deal of understanding, though in private Westmoreland agreed with much of my thinking about the fallacies of the limited-war strategy.

In public it was a different matter. Westmoreland had to be a diplomat as well as a soldier and he always played his cards close to his chest. It was hard to know what he really felt, because like all the Americans, so far from their homeland, he had to be sensitive to public opinion thousands of miles away.

Westmoreland was, unfortunately, not a man to capture the imagination of the people back home in America. He lacked the magnetic personality necessary to become a kind of folk hero who could have swung public opinion behind the war. The Americans need that kind of folk hero; they tend to see a war through the figurehead who is fighting it for them.

I do not suppose this is a uniquely American characteristic but it is particularly pronounced in America because of its mass media. Douglas MacArthur, with his corncob pipe and his crumpled cap, was a perfect example of the American military hero. He fought a long and bitter war in which Americans died on distant shores; yet he was such a dynamic personality he carried public opinion with him. What is more, he could stand up for his beliefs and defy the president even though it meant his dismissal.

I believe that if Westmoreland had come into the category of people like MacArthur, I would be writing this book in Saigon and it would have a different story to tell. We would have had the full support of the American people. We would have defined the politically imposed concept of a limited war and then, since attack is always the best method of defense, we would have won.

As it was, Westmoreland fought with his hands tied. How can you win a war if you are restricted politically in the action you can take militarily? It was like fighting in handcuffs.

I proposed to President Johnson in 1966 that, even though he insisted on a limited war, we should have at least one volunteer force to hold an area in the North, and I offered to lead it. After all, the Communists had their "safe areas" in the South, where they lived in our country; there seemed no reason why we should not do the same. No American need have been involved in the fighting; all I asked was assistance with fire power and supplies, but all my requests were refused.

Again in 1970 when we sent Vietnamese troops into Cambodia we tried to cut off three North Vietnamese divisions—the Fifth, Seventh, and Ninth—that were building up for an attack against us from the safety of a neutral country. When our tanks arrived the North Vietnamese withdrew before we could bring them to battle.

The following day we had a meeting with the Americans at the presidential palace and I proposed the obvious move—to drop paratroops behind the North Vietnamese so that, with our tanks in front, they would be encircled. The American answer was: "We must not go more than twenty-one miles inside Cambodia." Twenty-one miles had been sanctioned; twenty-two miles was beyond limits. Even the incursion that had been made into Cambodia rocked the Nixon administration; there was a massive backlash of public opinion in the United States and the Senate barred any further military operations in Cambodia without congressional approval.

As a consequence, those three North Vietnamese divisions that might have been destroyed were allowed to escape, and they were the same divisions that were to lead the final attack on Saigon.

Many actions that were banned because of the desire not to escalate the war had eventually to be taken later at an increased cost. Such was the case with the bombing of the North. I never felt that bombing could end the war. I told Secretary of State Dean Rusk on one occasion, "The more you bomb them the more you stiffen their morale and the more troops they will send South."

But having taken the decision to bomb the North, the Americans should have done it more wholeheartedly. At Guam in 1967 I pointed out to President Johnson on a map several airfields in the North from which Russian MIGs were operating. "Those are the targets that should be bombed," I said.

Johnson turned to Defense Secretary Robert McNamara and said, "Mac, tell the vice president why we cannot bomb those airfields."

McNamara replied, "We studied the possibility but the trouble is that those airfields are extremely well defended by flak and if we tried to attack them we would suffer enormously heavy losses."

That was possibly true and public opinion in America might well have been horrified by such losses, but I believe there was a political reason as well. In the end Americans had to go in and destroy those very airfields. What a pity it was not done earlier.

President Johnson also refused to consider my suggestion in 1966 that we should mine the harbor at Haiphong, although General Taylor endorsed it publicly. If we could have closed the port, it would have helped us greatly, but the president then feared reaction in Moscow and Peking that might follow the involvement of Russian and Chinese shipping.

Yet in 1972 Haiphong harbor was finally mined on President Nixon's orders.

I used to say to Westmoreland: "We can never win the war this way, when we are not allowed to fight as we should." On one occasion he replied, "It's tough, I see that. I know your way is best, yet I feel that we have enough strength and I'm confident that in the end we'll win out."

Maybe he really believed what he said. He was always optimistic and so was McNamara until disillusionment set in. But in their statements to the public they over-simplified a highly complex war and tried to please public opinion with promises that could not be fulfilled, and in the end the people of America did not trust them any more.

This was one of the penalties for trying to control a war from afar, and the Americans might have learned a lesson from their own history books, from the War of Independence, which began as a protest by the American colonists against taxation by the British crown and flared into open rebellion in 1775. The British fought that war for eight years from a distance of 3,500 miles until they were forced by the combined strength of the colonists and the French to accept American independence.

In Vietnam the Americans tried to wage a war at more than twice that distance. There was a saying in Saigon that "the Communists can win the war in Washington," and in a way they did, because in the end the Vietnam war was so unpopular in the United States that it became impossible for any administration to continue it, whatever the rights and wrongs of the American presence in Indochina.

The tragedy is that if the Americans had gone all-out in an attack on the North earlier, nothing could have prevented victory. They had the air power, the fire power, and the man-power to smash Hanoi to its knees, but this was not permitted. Nor were we allowed to try the alternative of pulling out a large proportion of the American troops, but keeping the fire power and letting our South Vietnamese officers take command, so building up the morale of our army and of the civilian population as well.

Never were the shortcomings of the "wrong army" policy more evident than when the Americans went into action against the shadowy National Liberation Forces. You cannot use a steamroller against a shadow. The Americans found themselves pitted against an enemy they could neither understand nor combat. When they raided a village suspected of harboring NLF they would find only women, children, and old men; the NLF had been swallowed in the jungle. Sometimes the Americans found bunkers crammed with explosives, medical supplies, and radios. Sometimes they found NLF caches of rice. But they pursued an elusive enemy who struck back unexpectedly.

If the Americans struck too hard at a suspected NLF stronghold their actions rebounded on them, for if the area was not in the hands of the NLF before, the resentment would make it easy for the NLF to convert the peasants. Gradually the NLF built up safe areas in the South.

We not only had the wrong army, but other factors contributed to defeat. If you do decide to fight a limited war— as Russia and China had—then get out of the way, do your work behind the scenes, never pose for a photographer, never give the world a picture that might be interpreted wrongly. There was no chance of that with Russia or China. Whoever saw a picture of those two mighty backers of Ho Chi Minh "advising" the North Vietnamese? Yet their sophisticated weapons, their latest MIG aircraft, their money, was pumped into North Vietnam in quantities that were truly colossal. The average soldier in North Vietnam had no idea of this. He was not fighting side by side with a Chinese who gave him advice or orders. All he knew was that "Uncle Ho" had found him a new rifle.

People sometimes looked askance when I cited Ho Chi Minh as the perfect example of a leader, but none can deny that he inspired his people. The morale of the North Vietnamese fighting man was based on worship of Ho and not on that of the Chinese or the Soviets who supplied him with arms. In our case the Americans kept too much in the foreground of the picture, as I told President Johnson.

Even the Americans agreed with my point of view. When President Johnson, always anxious to demonstrate direct American involvement in the battlefield picture, suggested on one occasion introducing "military-civil affairs personnel into the air effort," Ambassador Maxwell Taylor was so horrified that he cabled McGeorge Bundy in the White House, "Mac, can't we be better protected from our friends? I know that everyone wants to help, but there's such a thing as killing with kindness."

American over-exposure often had dire effects on morale. The average South Vietnamese soldier felt, because of our secondary role, that we were fighting for the United States in a war now America's. I remember hearing a man ask: "Why should we fight? The Americans are doing the fighting for us. Let's relax."

This was a feeling that crept insidiously into the Vietnamese over the years. And though the Americans were first-class soldiers and had courage and a sense of duty, they also lacked motivation. They had been drafted to fight a war in a far-off country. If one works and fights for a cause, an ideal, considerations like pay and comfort do not matter. This was an essential difference between the forces of North and South Vietnam.

The lack of American subtlety led not only to deteriorating morale among our troops but to grave consequences in world opinion and open hostility in the Third World where the war in Vietnam took on a sinister aspect. The view in newly liberated countries in Africa was one of mighty America attempting to crush a small Communist country. The picture was distorted because America was so much in the foreground.

World opinion soon narrowed into sharper focus: American public opinion. Never since the Civil War had the American nation been so torn apart. Yet consider what might have happened: if America had gone in to win outright, the smoke of battle would have cleared before the American people stopped rubbing their eyes. Or if the Americans had offered their skills, weapons, know-how as discreetly as the Russians did, the conscience of America would never have been tortured.

One other factor contributed enormously to American public opinion and thus, directly, to our defeat. Ours was the world's first TV war. For though the war was fought in Vietnam, it was refought nightly in the living rooms of the world, and that was where its outcome was eventually decided. Thanks to communication satellites, Vietnam became the first war in history in which the day's battles were screened globally by television the same night. The film crew in Vietnam ate breakfast, then caught a helicopter to the war to film their daily quota. The film was flown to Hong Kong, processed, then "birded" (satellited) across the world to be seen in far-away New York, Paris, and London that night, in color.

This television coverage was one of the principal weapons of our destruction, for it shocked American public opinion by unwittingly painting a picture of total war when America was committed to fighting only a limited war. If America had been helping us out of sight, the TV cameras would never have wasted their time in far-off Vietnam. If America, on the other hand, had decided on all-out war, the duration of the grisly catalogue of brutality that is a part of modern war would have been much shorter. Either way, we lost out.

I have no quarrel with the camera crews. Traveling with the army of one side in a conflict, they showed its bravery and hardships, but television also had to show an army fulfilling its basic purpose—destroying the enemy. Shots of Americans using flamethrowers and napalm horrified many at their dining tables. Of course, they did not see the North Vietnamese using them.

Shots of American flak ships with stuttering guns and bombers raining down their lethal cargoes tended to inspire sympathy for the apparent underdog. Yet in 1972, when Hanoi was complaining about half a dozen civilian casualties from an American raid, its own troops were pouring rockets into Saigon indiscriminately. When refugees fled from Quang Tri the Communists strafed them on the roads. This was permissible to Hanoi and its sympathizers; the American bombing was not.

Television pictures persuaded the general public that mighty America was bombing North Vietnam into oblivion. In fact, most bombing was of targets in jungle and swamp land and in no way comparable to the devastation unleashed on German cities by the American and British air forces in World War II.

The cameras could not be everywhere, but by following individual units television showed a "sampling" of the action rather than the overall picture. I was made aware of the shocked reaction when television showed my chief of police, General Nguyen Ngoc Loan, executing a Viet Cong terrorist by shooting him through the head at pointblank range. Life being what it is, an isolated incident tends to be regarded as part of a pattern, of an official policy, especially when that impression is fostered by the propagandists of the North and accepted by those who were against the war in America and Europe.

For there was no similar coverage of Viet Cong atrocities, of which there were many. The world resounded with the name of My Lai, but few registered the name of Cai Be, where the Viet Cong murdered forty wives and children of local militia, or Dak Son, where they incinerated two hundred fifty Montagnards—most of them women and children—with flamethrowers.

As Lyndon Johnson said after his retirement, "Showing the suffering and the savage combat was the price we paid for a free press." It was certainly a heavy price for South Vietnam, for in the end the blood, in color, on their television screens night after night, alienated many in the West and sickened the rest to such an extent that the Americans had to pull out. Certainly it was television more than any other factor that created the climate for the Paris peace talks and America's decision to cut adrift from us.

Once more I reiterate that we needed America; we could never have fought the Communists alone. But how much better it would have been if the Americans had never appeared in the picture and we had combined patience with American economic aid and expertise to improve the lot of the average Vietnamese family and the skill of our fighting men. I am convinced that slowly but surely we could have won the war, simply because all the people would have been behind us once the social revolution had been won.

14

TET:

The breaking of America's morale

By 1967, when my term as prime minister was drawing to a
close, I had to make a momentous decision. Earlier in the year,
after I had paid a visit to Australia and New Zealand, the army
had indicated to me privately that they wanted me to run for
president under the new constitution, and I had agreed to do
so. Thieu had decided that he would stand against me. Thieu
had already submitted his own name and that of Trinh Quoc
Khanh for president and vice president. As for me, I had
Nguyen Van Loc for my vice president. This posed a problem:
Thieu and I were both military men, and if we competed for
the presidency it might be interpreted as indicating a rift in the
armed forces. So Defense Minister General Cao Van Vien called
a meeting of the forty-eight general officers comprising the
Armed Forces Council. After a day or two of deliberation they
thought they had found a way out; they would retire Thieu
from the army and he could run against me as a civilian.

But Thieu was a smart tactician. When they told us the
proposal, he knew that as a civilian he would lose, so he declined to accept retirement.

After a day or two of deliberations and some very sharp
disagreements, the Armed Forces Council held a last summit
conference to reunite all members. About forty high-ranking
officers waited downstairs for a final decision to be taken in
an upstairs room by the seven highest members of the Committee of National Leadership. Thieu and I were both sitting
outside. I learned later that the Committee of National Leadership produced several alternatives. The main one consisted of

155

demobilizing Thieu, who could then run for the presidency as a civilian.

Thieu immediately realized that as a civilian he would stand no chance, and declared: "I still belong to the armed forces, and you cannot retire me."

I suddenly felt a surge of bitterness—not anger, more a feeling of sadness at the chicanery of politics. How despicable it all was: I had never really liked politics even though I had been prime minister. But I had lived through months of challenge for supremacy, disputes over functions and titles, and I was suddenly disgusted—disgusted and tired. In one split second, it dawned on me that, here we were, brothers-in-arms, tearing each other apart for the sake of power. What an example for officers to set for Vietnamese soldiers! I was sick and tired of the constant disputes between high-ranking officers since the overthrow of Diem. Depressed and fed up, I announced without warning to everyone present that they should lend their support to Thieu. "If Thieu wants to be a military candidate, let him. I'm going back to my job in the air force," I said.

There was a moment of stunned silence, finally broken by General Hoang Xuan Lam, commander of First Corps, who cried, "Since you are already making a sacrifice to help the unity of the armed forces, why not make it all the way? If Thieu runs alone, he may not win the race over the civilian contenders. But if you will run with Thieu as vice president on the ticket, your prestige will help to get our man elected."

I replied that if this was the wish of the council, I would agree, and run as vice president under Thieu, but I made it clear to the Armed Forces Council, who gave me a standing ovation, that the purpose of my sacrifice was to prevent further disputes which could break down military morale.

My gesture led the Committee of National Leadership to make a fundamental decision, making it certain that if we were elected, Thieu would have to obey the military, and I would have a share of power, not normally allowed under the constitution. The generals decided to form a secret organization, with a non-constitutional framework, called the Military Council. It embraced all the generals and high-ranking officers, as well as the minister of defense, the president, and the vice president.

The Military Council had the right to set up national policies, promote military and civil officials in the government, while any member of the Military Council who was elected president of the country would have to observe directives outlined by the chairman of the Military Council. In other words, the Military Council was organized beyond the boundaries and scope of the law. This underground "politburo" was to be the center of policy-making for all the armed forces; it had control over the military and the government as well. As chairman, I would actually hold more power and authority than the president.

As all the world knows, we were elected with only 33 percent of the ballots. It is unjust to call the election rigged. The public knew that I was extremely powerful and could have easily won with 60 or 70 percent of the votes if I wanted to cheat. I was the very person who organized and controlled the election; there was no reason for me to cheat in favor of Thieu and get the blame, when I had given up my own chance for the presidency.

Thieu cunningly grabbed more power for himself over the years, and sidestepped the Military Council. Many people thought my decision had serious consequences for the destiny of Vietnam, and later many people blamed me, as they saw more and more evidence that Thieu's blatant corruption had finally led South Vietnam to defeat. When I landed in the United States as a political refugee at Camp Pendleton, many Vietnamese still said the loss of South Vietnam was due partly to my withdrawal from the presidential race in 1967. With hindsight I can see the truth in their criticism. I should never have ceded power to someone so unworthy. I must take the blame. It is the error I most regret in my entire military and political career.

Vietnam boasted the finest presidential palace in all Asia, rebuilt on the site of the old French palace that was destroyed when Diem was overthrown. It was as large as the Washington White House and stood in superb grounds. Inside were private apartments for our family. However, I had decided to continue living at my office-cum-house at the air base. It had been a part of our lives since we married, and Mai could not bear to leave it. I did, however, have a large office near the president's and commuted from the base in my helicopter.

At first I landed on a helicopter pad on the palace roof, not knowing that it was directly over President Thieu's fourth-floor bedroom. And Thieu was a late riser. Thieu never mentioned the matter but finally his wife brought the subject up in a roundabout way, saying that she was making a beautiful roof garden so that she could take advantage of any breeze on warm evenings. "But," she said sadly, "I'm afraid it's going to be impossible. The enormous rush of air when your helicopter lands on the roof is ruining the plants."

Of course I landed in the palace grounds after that. But it was typical of Thieu that even if the noise wakened him, he would not mention the matter himself, but used his wife.

I had plenty of work. Apart from the formal functions of the vice president I played hookey whenever I could—but not to rest. Whenever I had time to spare I jumped into my helicopter and flew out to spend a few hours with isolated troop units.

By the end of the year the Americans were bombing the North heavily, though in his State of the Union message on January 17, 1968, Johnson promised—as he had done before— that American bombing would cease if talks were arranged promptly and with a reasonable chance of being productive. The Viet Cong's response was an upsurge of activity. They made a massive attack on the American marine base at Khe Sanh, fourteen miles south of the demilitarized zone. Then came the Tet offensive, named after the Vietnamese New Year. Savage, brilliantly executed, it caught all of us off balance. Almost before we knew what happened, we were fighting for our lives in the streets of Saigon, Hue, and a dozen other cities.

The Tet offensive marked a turning point in the war and in America's attitude to it. Before Tet the war had seemed to be receding as we pushed the Communists back into jungle north of the border. The previous November they had agreed to observe a holiday cease-fire at Christmas and at Tet as they had done the year before. But there were warning signs: on January 29 the Allies canceled the scheduled truce in the First

Corps area because of a big Communist build-up observed near Khe Sanh.

Nevertheless, when the Communists launched their attack in the early hours of January 31, nearly half the South Vietnamese soldiers were away from their units on vacation. And though General Frederick Weyand, commander of the U.S. Third Corps, had put his troops on alert the previous night, there were few American troops stationed in the cities. That was where the attacks came.

A combined force of 50,000 to 80,000 Communists launched a synchronized and coordinated onslaught on virtually every major city and town in the South. They struck at Saigon, Hue, and a hundred other places shortly before three in the morning.

In Saigon a suicide squad of nineteen NLF commandos blew their way through the outer walls of the American embassy and rushed the doors. Other squads attacked the presidential palace, the Joint General Staff headquarters, the South Vietnamese naval headquarters, the air base, and the radio station.

Thieu was out of Saigon and as vice president I took charge. At 4 A.M. the commander of the air base told me: "The Communists are even inside the base. I don't think I can stop them much longer; you and your family should leave."

I told him: "I am not going to leave," and I called my wife, children, and servants and gave them guns so that we could fight to the end.

Before long the Communists had occupied the radio station, but it was vital to get a message to the people to order a curfew and keep the streets clear so that we could deal with the enemy.

Somehow I made contact with the Saigon chief of police and told him, "I don't care how you do it, what you do, but that radio station must be in our hands by dawn. Let me know when you are ready; then I want to broadcast."

Over the crackling phone he shouted, "You can't! You can't get through the streets."

"That's my problem," I shouted back.

I *had* to broadcast, for half the people in Saigon had no inkling that this was a Communist offensive. The NLF were broadcasting their plans to overthrow what they called "the Thieu–Ky puppet regime"; and this lent credence to the belief, shared by many, that this was just another coup.

About 6 A.M. the police chief phoned me. He was launching a counterattack on the radio station.

"Is it in our hands?" I shouted.

"Not yet, Sir," he replied, "but it will be by the time you get here."

I jumped into my jeep and tore through the streets to the heart of the city. It was hell—that is the only word to describe what I saw. Pilots perhaps tend to take a rather remote view of hand-to-hand fighting, but now I was not above, looking down. I was in the thick of it, crunching over broken glass, skidding as I tried to avoid bodies littering the streets or the fires that seemed to blaze everywhere. Tearing around a corner I came across a group of men—three or four, it is all blurred in my memory—stabbing ferociously at some women and children. I was upon them before I could draw my revolver, so I ran down the men. I could feel the jeep bump and slither as I ran over them. One girl was still alive. She leapt into the jeep as it slowed up at the moment of impact with the bodies. I noticed only the blood pouring through her dress as I tore away. Behind me a Viet Cong survivor opened up with his sub-machine gun, and I could hear the *ping* as bullets hit the jeep, but no serious damage was done.

Even as I reached the radio station heavy fighting was still in progress. But the entrance had been cleared and, ordering someone to look after the girl, I dashed up the steps past the sprawling bodies of more dead soldiers. Two sergeants with automatic weapons led me into a studio. Almost as I reached it an officer rushed in. The last of the enemy had been killed and the station was in our hands again. It was 6:45 A.M.

With an almost exaggerated nonchalance a young mechanic tested the microphone, placed it carefully before me, and I made up the broadcast as I went along, telling everyone to stay in their homes while we dealt with the Communists.

By 9 A.M. American helicopter-borne forces had cleared

their embassy but elsewhere the fighting went on grimly. Saigon had seen nothing remotely like it since the Committee of the South had been ejected by the British, French, and Japanese in 1945; this was on a much bigger scale.

The Americans ringed the city, barring both escape and the bringing up of Communist reinforcements; then the Communists shelled Saigon itself. After five or six days there were still about 1,000 Communists fighting in the city, while in Hue it took until March 10 to liberate the city completely. The casualties were heavy: some 4,000 Americans were killed, together with 5,000 South Vietnamese troops and 5,000 civilians; over 34,000 Viet Cong were killed. For the first time the guerrillas of the National Liberation Front, who normally were careful to avoid harming civilians on whose goodwill they depended, resorted to terror tactics. They murdered some 3,000 civilians, including anti-Communists and Catholics. The bodies were found in three shallow graves, one in Hue and two on the outskirts of the city, some of them apparently deliberately executed, because their hands were bound behind their backs.

But tragic though this was, the biggest casualty of all was America's pride and prestige. To the Americans Tet had all the horrors of another Pearl Harbor, and for the first time many Americans realized that they might not be able to win the war. There was a shattering loss of confidence. The excuses began. Westmoreland declared: "Even though by mid-January we were certain that a major offensive action was planned by the enemy at Tet we did not surmise the true nature or the scope of the countrywide attack. . . . It did not occur to us that the enemy would undertake suicidal attacks in the face of our power."

That just isn't true. Of course Westmoreland must have known all about the strength of the impending attack. I am convinced the White House did not, but that was for a very good reason. It was clear that some of the American leaders in Saigon deliberately issued a string of lies to the White House, in an effort to maintain the impression that the Americans were getting on top of the Viet Cong.

It took some years to uncover this squalid deception before CIA analyst Samuel Adams, a specialist in Viet Cong troop strengths, disclosed* that the Americans had issued deliberately misleading estimates of Communist forces before the offensive. He said that though intelligence reports indicated the Communists had about 600,000 troops, the U.S. Command in Vietnam and the American ambassador in Saigon insisted on halving that figure for the press, Congress, and the White House. Adams produced cables from General Creighton Abrams, who had replaced Westmoreland, and Ambassador Ellsworth Bunker to substantiate his testimony.

Thus when the CIA predicted the Tet offensive two months in advance, it still quoted the out-of-date figure of 300,000 Communists and accordingly suggested that the attack would be smaller than it was. "Although our aim was to fool the American press, the public, and Congress, we in intelligence succeeded best in fooling ourselves," Adams admitted.

In fact, about a week before the attack, we ourselves discovered a cache of Russian AK47 rifles in Saigon and General Nguyen Ngoc Loan, the chief of police, ordered a state of alert and had 85 percent of his police on duty when Tet erupted. Maybe we were at fault in not taking the advance warnings seriously enough, but it is not always easy to argue with a senior partner.

At the beginning of the Tet offensive we were unable to get immediate help from the Americans. In the past, whenever there had been a battle, the Americans reacted with great speed, but during the Tet they adopted a strange "wait and see" attitude. We began to wonder about the depth of their commitment and whether they were really determined to win the war.

Later the American commanders and politicians revised their official view of the Tet campaign and tried to represent it as a victory. Westmoreland said it was a victory because the Viet Cong never took any city but Hue and they suffered crippling losses. This was true, but the American people never regained

---

* Before a congressional investigatory committee in September 1975.

their confidence in the outcome of the war. To Americans Tet was only a victory in the sense that Dunkirk was a victory for the British in World War II.

Yet, there is another irony. In a way, Tet *was* a victory for us —or would have been had we struck back. The great tragedy of Tet is that though the Americans never recovered from the blow, the North Vietnamese losses were so great that I believe we might have been able to inflict serious blows had we been allowed to go over to an immediate counterattack. If only my pleas to President Johnson to let us take offensive action had been answered! In the Tet offensive Hanoi lost 30 percent of its top-ranking junior officers in tactics so suicidal that even General Giap has admitted that his casualties, including deserters, in 1967 and 1968 numbered more than half a million men.

As Robert Thompson, a leading British authority on counterinsurgency, points out in his book *Peace Is Not at Hand*: "That would have been equivalent in the United States to losing an army of about five million men.... As subsequent events showed, the Vietcong were broken as a military threat and the North Vietnamese Army did not recover for two years."

While the Communists were reeling, we were burning with rage at the outrages at Hue and other cities, and ready to have a go. Though it is true that the South Vietnam Army had been trained by the Americans for defensive rather than offensive action, I still think we could have mauled the enemy.

It was not to be. My role in the aftermath of Tet was to chair a National Recovery Committee set up to distribute emergency relief, a major task as we had 200,000 homeless in Saigon alone.

But soon I had another less tangible duty: using my influence as I watched preparations for a political battle thousands of miles from our shores, yet one which could have profound effects on the destiny of our country—the American presidential elections of 1968, due to be held in an atmosphere of total American disenchantment with Southeast Asia and all it stood for.

15

THE PRESIDENT:

One reason why Nixon won

In a country whose morale had been shattered by the Tet offensive, the result of the 1968 presidential elections would have enormous effects on Vietnam. Already the American election scene was dominated by rumors of peace talks. No one wanted peace more than I did—but what kind of peace? Peace bought as part of a package deal in an election campaign? I did not need to be a political genius to know that any American presidential candidate who could pledge "peace with honor" on the Vietnamese issue would be hailed like a knight in shining armor from the Atlantic to the Pacific.

The signs of a possible sellout came dramatically almost before we had cleared up the shattered glass and buried the corpses in Hue. On March 31, Johnson decreed an end to bombing and naval attacks on North Vietnam, except in the area up to two hundred miles north of the demilitarized zone. Once more he called for a negotiated settlement. Then came the bombshell. Johnson announced that he would not stand for re-election as president in November so that he could remain above political infighting and respond to any feeler for peace.

No doubt deeply torn by the decision, Johnson had been warned by his advisers that even if he sent an additional 200,000 U.S. troops to Vietnam, as requested by Westmoreland, America would "not be in a position to drive the enemy from South Vietnam or destroy his forces."

Equally disturbing for Johnson was the shattering sense of despair among the civilian population of America, unable to comprehend that their army of half a million men could be so powerless against the North Vietnamese. The critics bellowed aggressively and as a draft memorandum by a group led by Clark M. Clifford, close adviser to the president, put it, "It will be difficult to convince critics that we are not simply destroying South Vietnam in order to 'save' it." The report went on to warn the president of civilian unrest, saying, "This growing disaffection accompanied, as it will be, by increased defiance of the draft and growing unrest in the cities because of the belief that we are neglecting domestic problems, runs great risks of provoking a domestic crisis of unprecedented proportions."

The die was cast. The North Vietnamese, whose strategy for years had been dominated by a resolve to break the will of America, to destroy its credibility in the eyes of the world, pressed home the advantage. The very next day the North Vietnamese government announced their willingness to discuss with the United States the total cessation of the bombing of Vietnam so that meaningful talks could start.

We were on the sidelines in these moves between the Americans and the North Vietnamese and were naturally suspicious of them, but even talks about talks were delayed by a disagreement about their location. The Americans proposed Geneva, Djakarta, New Delhi, Rangoon, and Vientiane and had them all rejected by the North Vietnamese. The North Vietnamese offered Phnom Penh and Warsaw and these were unacceptable to the Americans. Finally, on May 3, the Americans accepted Hanoi's proposal of Paris and named Averell Harriman and Cyrus Vance as their negotiators. The North Vietnamese named Xuan Thuy.

The talks about talks were to drag on for six months, largely because Hanoi demanded a complete halt to the bombing of North Vietnam before discussing a final settlement. South Vietnam did not attend these talks; the trouble was that the proposals were so vague. We did not know whether the substantive talks were intended to be between North and South Vietnam, or South Vietnam and the National Liberation Front, or America and North and South Vietnam, or all four parties, or more.

We had little desire to sit down with the Communists at all, and no intention of sitting down with, and thereby recognizing, the National Liberation Front. This organization, founded in 1960, was the political arm of the Communist effort in South Vietnam, though led by South Vietnamese claiming to be non-Communists.

However, Johnson quickly put pressure on us to go. Johnson and the Democratic candidate for the presidency, Hubert Humphrey, wanted the peace talks to succeed because American voters were becoming increasingly weary of the distant war, and a quick settlement could clinch the election for the Democrats. Johnson wrote personal letters to Thieu and to me, imploring us to agree.

Curiously, we never had any word from Humphrey. Though in the past he had supported Johnson's policy on the war loyally, his enthusiasm for South Vietnam seemed to cool shortly before the election. I have always been told that he is a very honest man and it seems to me possible that he changed his views because he realized his first loyalty must now be to the people rather than to the outgoing president. At any rate, I had reservations about the support we might get from Humphrey if he became president.

Then, out of the blue, Nixon's supporters stepped into the picture. Approaches were made to Bui Diem, the Vietnamese ambassador in Washington, to the effect: "Hold on! Don't accept the invitation to go to Paris. If Mr. Nixon is elected president he promises he will increase support for the Vietnam war."

In fact, Nixon was to campaign on a pledge to extricate the Americans from Vietnam but, of course, Johnson and Humphrey wanted a settlement *before* November 5, Nixon afterward.

All of this had no effect on our decision not to go to Paris, as it happened, though "Johnson's campaign" was soon flowing through Thieu's presidential palace. One day Thieu tried to bluff a joint American-Vietnamese communiqué through a meeting of the cabinet and the National Security Council. He and I had gathered with the prime minister, the minister of defense, and the chairmen of both Houses. Thieu outlined our problems with the Americans and then read us the communiqué, which none of us had seen. It was an agreement to go to Paris. If we signed it, he said, our difficulties with the Americans would be ended.

As vice president I sat next to him. "Let me see the communiqué," I said. He passed it over and I read it aloud again. Then I said, "We cannot accept this."

I explained why. It was too vague. It answered none of the basic questions, not even who the negotiations would be between. I told the assembled ministers, "We must know these fundamental matters before we agree to go to Paris."

And we refused to sign. Instead we voted that Thieu should call the American ambassador, Ellsworth Bunker, and restate our conditions, and this began a conflict with Bunker and his deputy, Samuel Berger, with whom Thieu had written the communiqué behind our backs.

Bunker, a former business executive, and Berger became the liaison officers conveying Johnson's desperate pleas for us to attend the talks. When the pressure mounted, Thieu and I spent two successive days and nights in the palace waiting for one or the other or both of them as they moved between palace and embassy. We worked through the nights until 5 A.M.

On the first night, when both the Americans were active, we had some soup brought in at 2 A.M. while we waited for new proposals from Washington for talks that would be acceptable to us. At 3 A.M. Berger took a tough line. "President Johnson has told us that if you do not agree to go to Paris he will order the bombing of North Vietnam ended immediately."

He said we were to sign a joint communiqué agreeing to halt the bombing and to go to the Paris talks. It was not a proposition; it was blackmail, and we refused. Berger went away and returned an hour later to repeat the threat. "If you do not accept, the United States will declare a unilateral end to the bombing."

I was too tired to argue any more. "It's up to you," I said.

Ambassador Bunker was not a bad fellow, though we had many differences, but I could never agree with Berger. Because of some shortcoming in his personality he failed to get through to the Vietnamese and had no rapport with any Vietnamese officials or military leaders. While I had my differences with Thieu, he was the president of an independent country, and no deputy ambassador should speak to or threaten a country's leader in the way Berger did. He probably thought he could impose his will on Thieu and, left alone with him, he might have been right. I saw that it did not happen.

The next morning Bunker came to see me privately in my office and carried on the pressure. "But President Thieu would never agree anyway," I told him, "so what is the use of talking to me."

"You know that Thieu will agree to anything to which you agree," Bunker retorted. This was partly true. In a way, Thieu used me. He liked to be on friendly terms with the Americans and to pretend that he was prepared to agree to a course of action if only his young upstart of a vice president could be made to toe the line. He knew perfectly well that I was not going to toe the line.

Events took their course. On October 31, five days before the presidential election, Johnson finally announced an end to the bombing and called for constructive four-party talks to end the war. He did this unilaterally and increased our fears that the United States was ready for a sellout.

It did not win the election for Humphrey. By holding out we deprived the Democrats of their election victory and Nixon became president instead. It is strange how a small country, so far away, could have such a profound effect on the destiny of a large nation. I wonder what might have happened if Humphrey had come to see us and reassure us of support. Who knows? We might have gone to Paris before the election and Humphrey could have told the voters, "I persuaded the South Vietnamese to talk peace," and I think he might have won.

Two days after Nixon's election Thieu made public the conditions under which we were prepared to go to Paris. They were that the talks should be two-sided between the Allies on one side, headed by South Vietnam and including the United States; on the other the Communists, headed by North Vietnam and including the National Liberation Front. In that way we would not have to recognize the NLF as a separate and equal entity. But Hanoi rejected this proposal. Xuan Thuy said they could not accept the concept of a single Communist delegation.

After another two weeks of wrangling, the American State Department obtained agreement that the Allied side would consist of separate delegations from the United States and South Vietnam and that the Communist side would, for practical purposes, be treated as a single delegation and that the presence of the NLF would not be interpreted to imply recognition of the NLF as a separate entity. And with this arrangement we concurred, since it resolved our main objection.

16

VIETNAMIZATION:

What's in a name?

For years I had begged the Americans to allow the Vietnamese Army to shoulder more responsibility, to have more say in the planning and execution of the war, for if one wants to build a great army there is no better kind of on-the-job training than fighting in the field of battle.

In view of the growing anti-war feeling in America, this also seemed an intelligent psychological move. Every American mother wanted her boy back home; but I also knew, from hints dropped to me, why the boys were remaining so long in Vietnam. The Americans did not think our troops were good enough to fight alone.

I remember asking President Johnson in Honolulu, "Isn't it possible for America to help us and yet keep out of the picture? Instead of making us look like the puppets of the giant Uncle Sam, let us fight the actual war. It will make us better soldiers."

Johnson said, "Yeah, we'll consider it." But I could sense that Johnson feared South Vietnam could never win the war.

When I later put the same question to Vice President Spiro Agnew, he answered more bluntly: "It sounds like a great idea, but do you think your boys can fight? I have heard reports they're not that good."

I had to admit, "You are partly right, but that is because they have been training and fighting for years as part of an American machine. Of course we need your equipment, but the morale of the armed forces would be much higher if our officers had more responsibility and felt they were fighting their own battle."

Agnew made some remark to the effect that this was not the whole problem.

"It is the root cause of all our troubles," I insisted. "Leave us alone and we will fight. Anyway, we don't have any time to discuss whether our troops are good or not. You know—even if you won't admit it—that public opinion will force you to pull American troops out of Vietnam, so surely the best thing for all of us is to do it right away?"

"Maybe you're right," said Agnew, "but I'm not sure you can do it that way."

The excellent American writer Robert Shaplen put his finger on the problem, when he pointed out in *The Road from War,* "It may be that the main thing we [America] have succeeded in doing in Vietnam over the past fifteen years—or, anyway, the last ten—has been to inhibit a natural revolutionary development that might have evolved on its own."

It was with very much the same thing in mind that, as guest of honor at a luncheon of nineteen former South Vietnamese generals in July 1969, I said, "The Americans have all along been wrong in their evaluation of the abilities and capacities of the Vietnamese people. According to reports by American advisers, a number of Vietnamese units are ineffective and it will be difficult for them to replace American units. But I told the advisers that when there is a possibility of our doing the job they should let us do it, so we can win the respect of the people."

Finally domestic pressure in the United States succeeded where I had tried in vain, forcing the Americans to hand over the fighting of the war to the Vietnamese. I went to Washington to discuss the program, and the first problem of the Americans—who like to label every project tidily—was to find a suitable name. At the Pentagon, Defense Secretary Melvin Laird asked the assembled group, "What shall we call the program?"

Someone suggested, "De-Americanization."

"No! for God's sake," I protested. "That would really prove to the world that you have been fighting the war." So, since it had always been our war, we settled finally on "Vietnamization."

The policy had been foreshadowed by General Westmoreland in 1967 when he told Americans on television that the United States might be able to start withdrawing some troops in 1969 if bombing and the military program on the ground continued, but this depended also on the capability of South Vietnam to assume a greater burden of the fighting.

Vietnamization was the keystone of President Nixon's Indochina policy. He had committed himself in his election campaign in 1968 to bringing the GIs home, but he calculated he could preserve a non-Communist regime in Saigon by bolstering the South Vietnamese forces. I had suggested the policy, and the idea had been supported by both Westmoreland and Abrams.

So he budgeted $10 billion for the job and General Creighton Abrams, who had succeeded Westmoreland as commander of U.S. forces in Vietnam in 1968, began a crash program to step up the training of South Vietnam's troops. We had already that year introduced general mobilization under which all men from eighteen to thirty-eight were eligible for military service and seventeen-year-olds and those from thirty-nine to forty-three could be called up to serve with village protection forces.

By the end of 1970 we had added 400,000 to our services and had 1,100,000 under arms.

General Frederick Weyand, Abrams' deputy, sent 350 five-man teams of U.S. advisers to train the regional and provincial forces that Americans called Ruff-Puff units. One hundred South Vietnamese soldiers flew out every week to the United States for training of from six to eighteen months duration. More than 12,000 South Vietnamese officers went for advanced training to the Command and General Staff College at Fort Leavenworth in Kansas, and to other bases.

In three years the United States handed over nearly a million light weapons, 46,000 vehicles, and 1,100 aircraft and helicopters.

Meanwhile the withdrawal of the American troops began.

In June 1969, Nixon announced that 25,000 of America's 541,-500 servicemen would be pulled out by the end of August as South Vietnam took on additional responsibility for the war. In September the second phase of the withdrawal was announced, and by December the total was down to 479,500 and the third phase was announced. In 1970 the number was reduced to 429,900, and by 1972, when the United States combat role ended, its troops were down to a mere 60,000, the lowest figure since mid-1965.

The task of re-making a new army out of one that had always been dependent on its partner for most of its commands, weapons, even strategy, was truly daunting. Over the years incidents in which I was involved brought the lesson home far more graphically than any theoretical treatise.

Our American allies never consciously tried to impose their way of life on Vietnamese officers, but it was inevitable that we had to adapt ourselves to the American way of fighting. I first realized the problems and dangers this involved from the moment when I became commander of the air force. I always felt that air power should normally be used sparingly, though overwhelmingly when necessary. But that was because Vietnam was a poor country. We had been educated to be almost miserly in the expenditure of ammunition. The American air force, with its vast budget, never gave this any thought.

I remember an occasion when a joint force of Americans and Vietnamese were advancing and ran suddenly into enemy resistance. The reaction was immediate; they called for an air strike to hit the enemy before advancing another step. We had to divert aircraft to attack the position, which was later found to have been held by half a dozen Viet Cong.

Yet two flights of Phantoms, each loaded with six bombs, costing, I am told, $1,000 each, were used and, even with that attack backed up by machine-gun fire, there was no evidence that we had killed any of the Viet Cong.

The squandering of ammunition was bad enough. But even worse, this dependence on ever-ready fire power led our generals into bad habits. After all, in a jungle war against guerrilla troops, air power can never be more than an aid. It plays a supporting role. In the last resort it is the infantryman, the jungle fighter, who gains the ground. But the availability of air power made life easier, and sometimes we were flying 5,000 sorties a day to support ground troops.

I was so concerned about what would happen to our morale when the Americans pulled out that I warned Thieu, "Don't imagine we will have the same kind of fire power as we have now when the Americans leave."

In fact, the Americans were later highly critical of Vietnamese ground forces for their reluctance to advance without air cover, yet it was they in their lavish use of it who taught our troops to expect it.

Then again, with the advent of Vietnamization, we had to reorient the thinking of men who had fought side by side with allies who had incredibly different standards of living, which created innumerable problems that we now acquired as a legacy. No one could blame the GI for eating well, for having the PX with all its duty-free goods, but when a Vietnamese unit operated closely with an American one, inevitably the Americans, who are the most generous people in the world, started doling out unlimited ice cream and cigarettes. The result was that every Vietnamese unit devoted all its energy to working alongside Americans, and when they were suddenly on their own, they missed all the American luxury.

How could it be otherwise? I saw once in a lonely jungle outpost how the Americans took showers. There were no shower facilities for at least twenty miles but with American resources this was no problem. A hundred Americans stripped and stood in a group. A helicopter came over and sprayed them with water. A second helicopter came over and sprayed them with liquid soap. Five minutes later, after they had all lathered themselves, the first helicopter returned to rinse them with another spray of water.

Another time my wife and I visited a lonely American outpost near the Laotian frontier. Up in high, rocky mountains the Americans had an artillery base to protect their troops below. Even as I jumped out of my helicopter to shake hands with the American commanding officer I sniffed good cooking. Miles from anywhere there was an American cook in a white apron and a chef's tall white hat, cooking mountains of steaks, tasty enough and plentiful enough for any rich man's table.

The Americans had every right to supply their soldiers with frozen steaks by helicopter, but our two armies lived in different worlds, yet close to each other. It might have been less difficult to train a new, Spartan army if the Vietnamese had been allowed more leadership earlier.

Whatever the faults that would later bring the world of Nixon crashing about his ears, he did have guts and determination, for after his 1968 election he might have been tempted to run for cover and try to go down in history as the man who got America out of the war immediately. But Vietnamization was a gradual process. As he said in one of his major policy speeches, "The precipitate withdrawal of all American forces from Vietnam would be a disaster, not only for South Vietnam but for the United States and the cause of peace."

He did, however, want to change the type of war America was waging, and this was a policy I heartily endorsed—one in which America at last realized that this was a Vietnamese war, in which the Americans should lend assistance rather than dominate the stage.

The trouble was that President Nixon found it almost impossible to get anywhere with President Thieu. The words "Yes" and "No" seemed absent from Thieu's vocabulary; or if not absent, they meant little more than a vague nod or shaking of the head, to be ignored as soon as the interview had been terminated.

So it fell to me to help formulate and explain to the people the two great issues that now loomed before our nation; not only Vietnamization but the peace talks that we knew would have to be held eventually.

I liked to point out, even at small village meetings, that Vietnamization did not concern only the armed forces. It ranged over the entire structure of the country: from the increasing production of rubber and rice, the growth of more livestock, including pigs, chickens, and ducks, the move to more mechanization on the land, to the wider, fairer distribution of that land.

It was not always easy, particularly as the Americans (understandably) tried to persuade me to take the long view. But as one unknown, resentful Vietnamese, quoted by Robert Shaplen, told an American, "It's fine to talk about long-term plans for agricultural production, forestry, fishing and so on, but we're in trouble right now. You've never thought of really teaching us instead of just building things."

As far as the peasants were concerned, Vietnamization had to start not at the top, but from the bottom up. After years of living under an American umbrella—and that could mean an American *driving* a tractor as well as explaining how it worked —the motivation was lacking. It was hard to explain to a South Vietnamese, whose aid had been a strictly material tractor, that he would reap a better harvest if he became part of an independent village instead of (as one American put it to me) "Holding hands with each other across the paddies." How often did I hear the simple, all-embracing question, "But if the Americans go, what happens when the tractor breaks down?"

I made it a priority to spread the word that we were not puppets of the Americans. I struggled to dispel misconceptions on subjects such as political prisoners. Hanoi propaganda claimed that the South held 200,000 political prisoners. This was nonsense; there were not even 200,000 prisoners of all kinds. We held some 27,000 prisoners of war, treated in conformity with the Geneva convention—and considerably better than Hanoi treated Americans in captivity.

The others, who totaled just over 30,000 at this time, included some 10,000 common criminals—thieves, gangsters, and the rest. Perhaps just over 20,000 were Communists, the great majority of them men tried and sentenced by provincial tribunals or military courts for terrorism, the others being suspects under investigation or awaiting trial. We held no more in detention or internment than any other country fighting for survival. Even the British have found it necessary to hold suspected terrorists without trial in Northern Ireland in recent years.

In fact, we dealt humanely with terrorists, for those waging war in civilian clothes have few rights in any country under any code of law. Yet we accorded prisoner-of-war status to many, while others served sentences of perhaps a couple of years, when they might well have faced firing squads. Exploding bombs in schoolrooms is not even warfare; it is murder, yet Hanoi and its sympathizers talked of "political prisoners."

Alexander Solzhenitsyn set out the cynical Hanoi thinking in an article on "Peace and Violence" which he wrote for the Oslo publication *Aftenposten* in September 1973: "When we are attacked, that is terrorism; when we do the attacking, that is a partisan freedom movement."

He also pointed out in connection with the Tet murders by the NLF: "The proven brutal mass murders in Hue are only noted in passing, almost immediately pardoned, because society's sympathy inclined to that viewpoint and no one wanted to go against this inertia. It was nothing short of scandalous that these accounts leaked out in the free press and for a [very short] time caused [precious little] embarrassment to the frenetic defenders of that social system."

As the Vietnamese began to take more and more responsibilities—whether in leading troops into battle or learning how to drive that tractor—we had our critics, but I did not mind. Healthy criticism was good for us, and good politically as I told Nixon when he visited Saigon in July 1969, during the Vietnamization program.

Nixon asked me one blunt question, "If there was a general election in which Communists were allowed to vote, would you, the Nationalists, beat the Communists?"

I said: "Yes, we would. And do you know why? Because, as you must be aware, Mr. President, our government has been under heavy criticism by both the national and foreign press. Ironically, that is the reason the Nationalists would win. The people of South Vietnam know that they still have the cherished right to criticize us, even to insult us, but Communism would never tolerate that, and that is why we would win in a free election tomorrow."

Nixon turned to an aide and said, "Give me a piece of paper

and a pen." Then he made some notes and put the paper in his pocket, saying, "Mr. Vice President, that's the simplest and clearest lesson I have ever had on how to win an election."

Occasionally I visited the United States for discussions at the Pentagon, sometimes combining these talks with other more normal duties of a vice president, as when I traveled to Washington to represent Thieu at the funeral of former President Eisenhower.

While there I had one unfortunate encounter and one happy one. After the funeral, Nixon gave a reception for all heads of state or their representatives. Among the guests was President de Gaulle, then approaching the end of his political life. Though I admired his patriotism I never liked him, and I could not bring myself to shake his hand. Indeed, I refused to do so, because his stated policy was always to make accommodations with North Vietnam. Apparently a newspaperman interviewed de Gaulle in Washington and asked the irascible general for his views on Vietnam. When my name came up, de Gaulle, attempting a feeble pun, asked sarcastically, "Qui est Ky?"

The reporter then came round to me and related the story. "What's your answer, Sir?" he asked me.

"Ky est Ky," I replied, "and he's younger than the general, he's more good-looking, and he's got a far more beautiful wife."

Hubert Humphrey had invited my wife and me to stay with him and, on the spur of the moment, after the funeral, he asked me, "Would you like to talk to former President Johnson?"

I was delighted. I had always liked Johnson. He was a Texan and maybe in a way I am a bit of a Texan myself. Certainly, when I was a youngster in Vietnam the only movies we saw were Westerns with the good guy—on a white horse—beating the bad guys. Somehow Johnson reminded me of those days and, equally on the spur of the moment, I asked him if I could visit his ranch.

I flew down next day. Johnson drove his station wagon to the airstrip to meet us and that night he gave us the finest steak dinner I have ever eaten. Diplomatic protocol usually prevents one from asking for a second helping but on this occasion it went out of the window as I asked, "Mr. Johnson, with your permission . . . ?"

All of us went through the meal a second time, then spent the evening on rocking chairs on the porch.

On one trip to Washington I decided to give a formal dinner for the diplomatic corps, and suggested to our ambassador that he invite Dr. Kissinger. With a barely concealed smile, he told me that Kissinger had made it a strict rule never to attend any official receptions. "Well, ask him anyway," I said, "he can only refuse."

He did refuse. He was then very close to Nixon and explained that he just could not get away from the White House. So the ambassador arranged the place settings according to protocol. We planned to dine on the outside of a huge U-shaped table so that everyone could see everyone else. I had Martha Mitchell, as the wife of the Attorney General, the highest-ranking American, on my right.

All was ready. Then at 4 P.M. Kissinger called me personally. He would like to come. Perhaps he suddenly remembered that happy-go-lucky lunch when, as a Harvard professor, he visited with us at Nha Trang. But where could we place him? Our ambassador was nearly in tears. Finally I solved the problem. Nobody was sitting on the inside of the U-table, so I ordered one place setting on the *inside* opposite me. Kissinger was delighted.

There was one slight *faux pas* before dinner. Mai and I were on the reception line, and when Kissinger arrived, Mai didn't recognize him! They looked at each other, then he said, "Madame, I am Dr. Kissinger. You don't remember *me*, but I will always remember *you* and that wonderful lunch at your home."

I had a less informal encounter with a cross-section of the youth of America when I stayed a night in the historic town of Williamsburg and found fifty or so youngsters gathered below my hotel window.

It was bitterly cold, and I asked the American Secret Service man who was guarding me what the trouble was about.

"They are protesting against you, Sir," he replied stolidly.

My wife came to the window, then I turned to the Secret Service man and said, "I would like to meet them. Ask them if they will come into the hotel lobby where it is warm. I will go down and talk to them with pleasure."

"No *Sir*, Mr. Vice President. You never know the reaction among these types; some of them take drugs...." He left the sentence unfinished.

Despite his protest I insisted, and finally the group of youngsters stood in the hotel lobby and I came down with my wife and asked them, "Now, what do you want?"

Very politely the spokesman said, "We are staging a silent protest against the war in Vietnam."

"So am I," I replied. "I want to stop the war as much as you do. I have been fighting this war for twenty-four years, risking my life every moment of every day. You can see that I have a beautiful wife. Here she is. I have a family. All I want to do is to enjoy life. So, more than any of you people here, I want peace. Without peace no one can enjoy life. I don't see why you should protest against me. I *know* what the war is about."

The trouble with young people today—and I can feel this because I am young—is that very often they only want to be told the answers. This was my first contact with the younger generation of America, my first chance to talk to them. I felt they were just kids; but they were eager to know. And when I was honest with them, the generation gap disappeared. I felt that they understood at the very least that I had a point of view.

Back in Washington, before flying home, I was invited to have a working breakfast with Nixon. How astute that man is! Unerringly he seized on the one single personal problem that had been worrying me for months—my deteriorating relations with Thieu.

As we were drinking a final cup of coffee, Nixon turned to me and asked, "What about the 1971 election in Vietnam?" No doubt he had heard that I was seriously thinking of splitting up with Thieu, and I assumed that he wanted confirmation. As I looked at him, wondering what to reply, he laughed and said, "Don't tell me. I understand. All politicians are in the same boat."

17

PARIS:

When the killing had to stop

For nearly a year I had vigorously opposed holding the proposed Paris talks because the North Vietnamese insisted that the National Liberation Front must be represented at the conference table. Even President Thieu backed me, declaring, "We will never set up a coalition government with the NLF and we will never recognize it as a political entity equal to us, with which we must negotiate on an equal footing."

Despite American and world pressure on us to go to Paris, we kept that resolve; we were determined never to recognize the presence of the NLF at the talks, only that of the Communist delegation headed by the Hanoi representative; even though by this time the NLF had gained widespread recognition. Prince Sihanouk of Cambodia had already started to negotiate with the NLF. Hanoi gave them official support by insisting that any negotiated settlement of the war would have to take into account the NLF's ten-point program. And I knew that the Americans were beginning to believe that the points could at least provide a basis for discussion, though if we ever accepted them, it would mean giving the NLF a free hand in South Vietnam.

Yet with each week that passed, I realized more and more that we could not continue fighting indefinitely. And apart from my own feelings of war weariness, the Americans were becoming more and more outspoken in their determination to end the struggle. So, at the end of 1968, I found myself in Paris heading South Vietnam's delegation to the peace talks.

The first real peace initiative had been made four years previously by U Thant, Secretary-General of the United Nations. He proposed reconvening the 1954 Geneva "partition" conference, but no one relished the idea—least of all North Vietnam, Russia, and China.

Early in 1965 U Thant tried behind-the-scenes diplomacy, but his disclosure that he had secretly contacted both North Vietnam and the United States in the hope of bringing about a graceful withdrawal by the Americans, was badly timed. It coincided with the very day the Americans launched B57 bombers and F100 fighter bombers manned by American crews for the first time against Viet Cong troops in Binh Dinh.

The United States reply to U Thant, when it came, merely thanked him for his suggestion and made it clear that there could be no peace until North Vietnam ceased its aggression in the South. Other pressures had come to nothing, as when seventeen non-aligned nations, meeting in Belgrade, called for an end of the war through negotiation. Sensitive to world opinion, Johnson did suspend American bombing of the North for six days to see if Hanoi would respond, but the Viet Cong continued to inflict heavy casualties on us and the Americans, and bombing was resumed of roads, bridges, and barracks close to Hanoi.

Johnson himself called for negotiations, claiming that America had sought fifteen times to get Hanoi to a conference table. He invited further help from U Thant and the United Nations. But at that time Hanoi was obviously bent on humiliating the United States and the war continued unabated.

Now we were in Paris. We had rented a villa in the Boulevard Maillot for the South Vietnamese delegation and it became, on and off for two years, a second home and a bustling office.

But before we would start the talks proper at the Hotel Majestic we had a month or more of preliminary discussions over the shape of the table, which had to be such that we could negotiate without recognizing the NLF.

Oh! That table. It was a bizarre battle. At least, it was bizarre to the press, but it was of fundamental importance to us. There was no way in which we were prepared to negotiate with the

NLF, who in our view were traitors, and therefore we insisted that the agreement not to distinguish the NLF as a separate party to the talks must be carried out to the letter—and this meant not sitting down "officially" with them at the same table.

After various-shaped tables had been proposed—and discarded—I think I helped to solve the table problem after Averell Harriman, head of the U.S. delegation, came to see me at our villa. I could see that the Americans were becoming irritated at what seemed to them a trivial obstinacy on our part, but Thieu himself had given me clear instructions not to give way on any account.

Harriman was a tough customer, and he had one very off-putting habit. He wore a hearing aid, and the moment he became disinterested or annoyed with a discussion, he signified his exasperation by ostentatiously switching off his hearing apparatus. When he arrived with a sketch for an oval table, and I said it was impossible, I saw his hand stray toward the aid. Like a conjuror, I produced four or five different sketches of tables and seating plans.

"Don't show them all to the North Vietnamese at the same time," I said. "Let them see one at a time. And this one"—I marked it with an X in pencil—"is the one we can accept. If you keep it to the last, and produce it as your idea, they might agree."

The ruse worked. After a month of farcical bargaining—with our trump card carefully hidden—Harriman suggested a circular table 26 feet wide, without nameplates, flags, or markings, for the chief negotiators, together with two rectangular tables, for others, 3 x 4½ feet, placed 18 inches from the circular table and at opposite sides.

To this day I am convinced that if Harriman had offered this suggestion first, it would never have been accepted by the North.

By this time it was mid-January 1969 but at last substantive talks could begin. With Nixon now in the White House, Harriman retired from the scene and a new American team headed by Lodge took over.

The blow-by-blow account of the long, dreary talks does not

bear repetition. From time to time, when all sides were bogged down, I flew back to Saigon to report; indeed, at one stage, I was almost commuting. What concerned me about the talks was the lack of reality, brought about by the very visible presence of America, but even more by the invisible presence of Russia and China, and I sometimes wondered if we could not achieve results more quickly if three or four of us from the North and South met around a table, drank tea, and offered each other enough concessions to bring about a peace that all wanted.

After some hesitation, and without informing Saigon, I decided to meet a top Communist from Hanoi secretly, to see if we could not discover one mutual base from which we could start discussions.

Thousands of Vietnamese of every shade in the political spectrum lived in Paris, and after two weeks of quiet inquiries by trusted intermediaries, the meeting was set up. I cannot to this day say where I went, for we met in the house of a friend of mine who still lives in Paris. I had to get there in the utmost secrecy.

As a cover, I made great play of the fact that I was taking my wife shopping. We set off from the Boulevard Maillot in the official car, trailed, no doubt, by the Secret Service and members of the press. We went in and out of a few shops, stopping finally at the Ritz Hotel, which has two entrances, one in the Place Vendôme, the other in the Rue Cambon. They are linked by the most exciting indoor shopping arcade in Paris, the perfect place for a woman to browse.

Once inside the Ritz, it required no great effort for me to give everyone the slip, leaving poor Mai as a decoy. At the Rue Cambon entrance I waited next to the small bar until a taxi drew up, then speeded off to my assignation.

For three hours we talked alone, two men from the opposite camps of war. I told my fellow conspirator, "I'm no more nationalist than you are. I love Vietnam—it's my country, but it's also yours. It's time to stop killing each other."

I remember the way he looked at me and said, "I am a Communist, but I am also a Vietnamese. I believe that if we were left alone we could write a ticket for peace in a couple of days."

I asked him what the major demand would be, and he never hesitated, not for a second. "Get rid of Thieu," he said. It was the first time I had heard direct evidence of the hatred in which Thieu was held by the Communists. The man spat the words out.

Leaning forward, he added, "If you could get rid of Thieu, I know we could reach an amicable compromise solution."

"Not so easy," I replied.

"For you? Of course it is. Why don't you go back to Saigon, overthrow Thieu, and then. . . ."

"I would do it," I agreed, "but only if I can have Hanoi's full agreement that if I come to power we can start talks immediately on a person-to-person level."

And this was where the plan broke down. He was "convinced" it would be all right, that I could "trust" him—but as for an official undertaking, that was not possible.

The phony shopping expedition caused a few ripples. The press accused me of being a reckless spendthrift (of my government's money, of course) and when they became tired of the word "shop" they substituted the word "nightclub."

What nonsense it all was. I did take Mai shopping—on one single, glorious spending spree, when I unexpectedly acquired a fistful of good old American greenbacks.

Since our villa was besieged day and night by reporters and cameramen, it was always difficult for us to go out, and one Friday Philip Habib, a State Department member of the American delegation, phoned me and asked what I was doing for the weekend. I explained the situation and he suggested, "Okay, let's play poker at your villa." We did. We played until 5 P.M. on Saturday evening, by which time Mr. Habib had no money left. Most of it was in my pocket, so I invited my wife to go shopping on the Champs Elysées.

That was an exception. Throughout our stay in Paris we had to be very careful to avoid giving the wrong impression. Though our communal delegation villa was far cheaper than a hotel, the press pretended that we lived in Oriental splendor. In fact, we had no money to spare.

The French magazine *Paris-Match* told my wife they would like to take a series of pictures showing how a beautiful Vietnamese woman looked in Western clothes. My wife explained to their reporter, "I don't have any Western clothes; we can't afford the prices of the big fashion houses."

"No problem," said the girl. "I will arrange with the leading designers to lend the clothes."

At this point my wife became worried and asked me if I thought it was all right. I said I thought it was a good idea, provided the article made it clear that the clothes had been lent for the pictures. But when the feature appeared there was no mention of the fact that the clothes were not her own.

I suppose much of the nonsense written about me in the American and European press stemmed from the fact that there was little to report from the negotiations and perhaps because I was a young man. Why otherwise did one newspaper announce that I could be expected to spend a great deal of my time in the nightclubs? Donald Wise wrote solemnly in the London *Daily Mirror* that "Ky is emotional, fond of roses, apt to read poetry tearfully to admiring ladies and, having swapped his black flying suit for a white tuxedo, will inevitably dance the frug in Paris with handsome competence. Not even Ky can frug back home because dancing has been banned in South Vietnam."

Poor Mr. Wise! I dance, I hope, with more than "handsome competence."

The American press was worse, branding me in turn as a military dictator, a dilettante, a Fascist, and (as a change) even an agent in the pay of Ho Chi Minh. Senator George McGovern made particularly senseless charges that I was nightclubbing around Paris, and had actually tried to delay the opening of the peace negotiations so that I could dally in the fleshpots of Paris while American boys were dying on the battlefields of Vietnam.

At what point do people like this stop? If I denied McGovern's stupid allegations, then I would sink to his slimy level.

Yet, if I didn't deny them, the world would believe the allegations were true.

I much preferred the considered judgment of the British journalist Ian Ward, "As far as Ky's credentials as a politico-military strategist are concerned, his choice as Saigon's top man in Paris can scarcely be criticised," adding, in a review of my term as premier, "Single-handed he moulded a form of political unity out of chaos and dragged his country from the brink of almost certain Communist takeover."

I was not sorry when the time came to leave Paris and return to the real world of Saigon and the war. The talks were not progressing fast; they could hardly have been expected to do so. They dragged on until March 1972, when they were suspended indefinitely and American bombing was extended. By then I was out of politics. The talks resumed again in July 1972, but the cease-fire agreements were not reached until January 1973.

The Vietnam war ended, so far as America was concerned, with the cease-fire at midnight on Saturday, January 27, 1973. Four nights earlier President Nixon appeared on television after the initialing of the agreement in Paris, to tell America that it had achieved "peace with honor." Within sixty days of the cease-fire, he said, all American troops would leave Vietnam and all United States prisoners would be freed by Hanoi.

Peace would achieve what America had fought for over so many bloody years, he claimed. "South Vietnam has gained the right to determine its own future."

"Ending the war," he said, "is only the first step to building the peace. All parties must now see to it that this is a peace that lasts and a peace that heals. This means that the terms of agreement must be scrupulously adhered to. Throughout the years of negotiations we have insisted on peace with honor. In the settlement that has now been agreed to, all the stipulations I have set down have been met."

He pledged to the leaders of North Vietnam that the United States was prepared to make a major effort to help it recover from the war.

But then came a sanctimonious passage which I could not

stomach, so nauseating was its hypocrisy and self-delusion.

"Let us be proud," cried Nixon, "that America did not settle for a peace that would have betrayed our ally, that would have abandoned our prisoners of war, that would have ended the war for us but continued the war for the fifty million people of Indochina."

Simultaneous announcements were made in Hanoi and Saigon, where President Thieu called for big American air strikes in a last-minute bid to recapture lost territory and prevent Communist infiltration into government-held areas. As a result, jets flew 374 bombing missions in support of ground forces and Hanoi protested angrily about the "war maniacs" of the South.

Officially the war was virtually over and the Americans were euphoric.

I could understand the American joy at extricating themselves from the war, particularly when figures were published setting out the cost of American involvement. Of the 2.3 million men who had fought over the years, 56,000 had died (though it should be remembered that South Vietnamese forces had suffered 165,000 killed).

American bombers and fighters had carried out more than 850,000 attack sorties and dropped more than 6 million tons of bombs, while helicopter attack sorties had averaged 2 million a year. This had cost them 3,695 aircraft and 4,783 helicopters.

In monetary terms the price of the war had been some $130 billion, without counting long-term interest payments on war debts and pensions.

But to me there was a strange impermanence about the result, and I think I felt that way because we had seen Kissinger in action before—and had seen how the much-heralded agreements so often broke down.

Much blood had flowed under the bridge since Kissinger lunched with us at Nha Trang, and of course no one can deny that Kissinger has a brilliant brain and many admirable qualities. Certainly, whatever project he is engaged on, America is always uppermost in his mind. But when he went into action (whether in Vietnam or the Middle East) he reminded me of a boxer. At the end of one round the bell rang and the fighting stopped. But even if Kissinger won that round, it did not mean he would necessarily win the fight. There was always the next round. Kissinger, however, was very adept at fighting a war round by round.

A small country like mine is always in a predicament when it is being helped by a large one. I am sure Kissinger knew that every cease-fire he tried to arrange—whether in my country or in the Middle East—was only temporary. To Kissinger the *simple* solution was always to fight for a *temporary* solution, in the hope that it might become permanent. Certainly for America—and for Kissinger personally—this resulted in a series of minor triumphs. But for us, the so-called allies, there were times, as Kissinger wheeled and dealed with one side or another, when we wondered whether we were only pawns, ready to be sacrificed if necessary to save America's global policy.

I was not deluded into believing that the Paris accord would bring permanent peace. By the time of the cease-fire agreement in January 1973, the NLF had already restyled itself the Provisional Revolutionary Government. Our foreign minister, Tran Van Lam, signed agreements only with North Vietnam's negotiator, Xuan Thuy, but there was a further session later in the day at which a modified agreement mentioning the PRG was signed by the Americans, the North Vietnamese, and Mme. Binh, foreign minister of the PRG. We refused to accept copies of that text, but there was no doubt that the NLF had won its biggest victory.

I felt certain the fighting was not yet over, as I told General Charles J. Timmes of the CIA, an old friend, who came to see me between the signing and the departure of the last American troops in March 1973. He asked me if the Communists would respect the promises they had given in Paris.

"Of course not," I told him. "They will not respect them because they have got the Americans out and that is the biggest victory the Communists have ever had. But it is not the first. They chased out the French and now, in a sense, they have chased out the Americans. That is an enormous step toward the total domination of Vietnam and there is no reason why they should stop now. The Communists in the North have always considered it a historical mission for them to achieve the unification of Vietnam."

I knew the Communists would not launch a major attack for some time. As I told Timmes, they had to take world opinion —even American public opinion—into account. But they would lose nothing by waiting; they had to make preparations before launching a final offensive and they could afford to wait after all the years of fighting.

In fact, the Paris agreement gave the world an entirely wrong impression. Though it *was* the end of the war for America, it was *never* regarded as the end of the war by Hanoi. At a moment when they desperately needed a respite to repair the enormous damage done in their country, the North Vietnamese seized on one fact: that the United States was not really concerned with peace at all; it was only concerned with getting out of Vietnam.

If the United States had really been determined to achieve "peace with honor," Nixon could have laid down onerous demands for concessions, and the stricken North Vietnamese would have been forced to accept. Nixon could have said bluntly to Hanoi: "Stop now or we will invade and bomb you." Hanoi would have had to agree, for the country was on the verge of starvation and total disruption. But Nixon could never publicly lay down that gauntlet. So the peace agreement was a sham, giving enormous benefits in time to Hanoi.

"I give them a couple of years before they invade the South," I told Timmes.

My doleful prophecy was not far wrong.

18

ALONE:

The promise Nixon could not keep

As the presidential election approached, and my four-year term of office neared its end, I made up my mind not to run for the vice presidency again—even had Thieu wanted me, which he no longer did. His choice was Huong, who had been his first premier and subsequently his secretary-general at the palace. I decided to run for president.

But the election was rigged. As I expected, there were two major contenders—Big Minh, back from the wilderness, and myself—but in four years Thieu had so consolidated his position that a really free election was impossible. He had made laws that rendered it difficult for any opponent to run, let alone win. Ho Chi Minh couldn't have done better.

Even to be accepted as a candidate one had to represent a major party (which I did not) or be introduced and sponsored by forty senators and congressmen. Thieu controlled them all. One hundred signatures were needed from members of the Provincial Council, but while I knew there were enough members who wanted me to run, Thieu had passed a law giving him power to dismiss them arbitrarily, and so placed them in a difficult position.

Thieu did everything to prevent opponents running against him. Members of his own intelligence service told me that 65 percent of the armed forces would have voted for me, or possibly Minh, in an honest election, but after four years Thieu controlled the police and, through the police, the people.

In a country where coups had become a way of life, it was inevitable that we discussed the possibility of an armed coup against Thieu. I knew I could rely completely on the air force and on most generals in the army, but secrecy was impossible because the last Americans were working in close contact with Vietnamese units. They would certainly have tipped off Thieu.

Many of the general officers insisted that we did not need troops. "Just get the top officers to sign an ultimatum and Thieu will go," one said.

But that was not possible. The general officers might be in favor of a change of government but the top brass, the officers who worked for the Joint General Staff, were each approached by Americans who warned them not to interfere, backing the warning with subtle bribery. I know of at least three members of the Joint General Staff who hated Thieu but—at a time when they knew nothing could save our country—they were approached by Americans with categorical promises that they would be looked after in the United States for the rest of their lives if they did not interfere.

For the Americans needed an atmosphere of political security in order to be able to withdraw their troops. In fact, Colonel Chau Van Tien, chief of the province of Gia Dinh, near Saigon, visited the air base and talked to the men one day when I was away, telling them, "We have heard rumors that Marshal Ky is planning a coup. If it happens, we are ready to fight it. We have American helicopter units standing by and a coup will never succeed."

In the end I decided that the interests of my country were best served by avoiding a military showdown with Thieu and, as always, I put those interests first.

Curiously, though the American State Department made it clear to me that they would brook no open conflict between Thieu and myself (anything even resembling a planned coup), they very much wanted me to oppose him in the election. They felt it would make the election look more democratic. Ambassador Bunker came to me at my home at the air base one afternoon and said, "A one-man show will not be a good example for the rest of the world." He even offered to find financing for my election campaign. He must have known that I would have no chance of winning, but presumably America felt the money would be well spent if it provided a façade of a free election.

The CIA also pressured me to stand but I told them, as I had told the ambassador: "It is impossible. Thieu has too tight a grip to allow me to succeed." In the end both Minh and I withdrew and the election went ahead with only one name on the ballot paper, that of Thieu.

On October 4, 1971, 6.3 million went to the polls, a turnout of 87.9 percent of the electorate. Some 356,000 handed in spoiled papers, many of them spoiled deliberately as a protest against the solitary candidate, but as nearly 6 million voted for Thieu he was elected by some 94 percent. It was a ridiculous election, like a Communist one.

So then, after two years as premier and four as vice president, I was out of a job. I still kept my rank of marshal, I still lived in the house at the air base, and I made frequent morale-boosting visits to troops all over the country, usually piloting my own aircraft. I still had Westmoreland's helicopter, and an aide-de-camp at my disposal, and Thieu gave orders I was not to be hindered in any way. He know that I retained the loyalty of the air force and I think he felt it best that I should carry on without authority and without specific duties.

I did just that, and after 1973 I often "commuted" to the farm in Khanh Duong, for I had my helicopter. Even when I was not at my house on the base, I kept in constant touch, for I had the finest civilian radio transmitting and receiving station in South Vietnam. When I decided to start our farm, American friends, who were kind enough to say they admired my political beliefs and were sorry to see me go, offered to install a communications center for me. They did. Isolated in the jungle, my radio was so powerful that I could not only talk to Mai and the children in Saigon, but even overseas.

There was a great deal of speculation when it was discovered that the set had been installed by Americans. One old friend came to me at the air base when I was down in Saigon and said, "What does the White House think of the trouble we're in?"

I looked at him, astonished. "How should I know?" I asked.

It was his turn to look surprised. "Well," he said, "I've been told that you talk directly to the White House on your jungle radio."

All of us who witnessed the sellout at the Paris talks had no hesitation in believing that it was now only a question of time before the North Vietnamese attacked us. They were in no hurry, for each day they waited meant a drop in South Vietnamese morale as we watched our one-time allies on their way back home—and, to them, peace.

The North Vietnamese also had to await the decision of their allies—Russia and China—for General Giap could not move a man without their approval, if only because the North Vietnamese were as dependent on Russian aid as we were on American help.

Indeed, the Communists could never have invaded us without massive aid from Russia, which for eighteen months had been pouring in the latest MIG aircraft, SAM missiles, T54 tanks, 130mm guns and mortars, together with trucks, ammunition, and—for the first time—the latest SA7 heat-seeking missiles which, when fired near a helicopter, were drawn toward it by the chopper's exhaust heat.

As the big push started—and until defeat—we read time after time stories of Vietnamese soldiers who panicked, ran away in terror now that they no longer had their American back-up. At times the newspaper stories were true—as true as they had been in France in June 1940—but, unfortunately, if the old saying is true that no news is good news, it is also true that good news is no news.

Looking back now, I like to think of the heroic stands that loyal and brave Vietnamese *did* make, especially in the Easter offensive of 1972.

I think of General Ngo Quang Truong, who rose from battalion commander to supreme commander of all forces facing the invaders crossing the demilitarized zone in the North. Author Robert Thompson regards Truong as "one of the finest generals in the world" and certainly he infused new life and vigor into the front. Nobody reported Truong's magnificent holding action along the entire DMZ until he was finally overwhelmed after refusing to retreat.

Nor have I read reports of the way in which our boys held Kontum, in the Central Highlands, for days after the government expected its defeat. Even the French, when fighting us, never attempted to hold Kontum, which lies in a valley dominated by hills, with only one road for reinforcements—or escape.

The legendary Colonel Ba and his men of the 23rd Division were surrounded by two Communist divisions, plus units armed with Russian tanks, 130mm guns, and B40 rockets. Even when the Communists poured into the outskirts and reached the Catholic Cathedral, turning it into an enemy stronghold, our troops held. The Communists sent in tanks. Still the South Vietnamese refused to acknowledge defeat. For four days they fought hand-to-hand inside the city, killing the enemy, man by man, in house by house, until the Communists had to retreat, leaving the carcasses of their burned-out tanks buried in the dust and debris of a city's defiant stand.

The same thing happened at An Loc. Though hardly a building was left in the city after the North Vietnamese fired 70,000 rounds of artillery fire, the troops defended the rubble, even against the Russian T54 tanks. As our men died while firing their antitank guns, policemen stepped forward to man them and fought on until barely 5,000 out of 20,000 defenders were left in the city. But they had won, for they had broken the backs—and the hearts—of three North Vietnamese divisions, the remnants of which skulked away. There were no newspapermen to witness *that* battle.

Criticism of our troops was also joined by bitter attacks on our "ineffectual air force" now that the Americans were leaving. More often than not they were written by journalists who never really attempted to discover *why* our planes were often on the ground instead of being in the air. Though I was no longer the head of the air force at that time—and so am in no way trying to defend myself personally—I reject those criticisms completely. They show a total ignorance of the situation which was brought about by problems that started when the first Americans arrived.

The usual form of criticism ran on these lines: America

pumped men and machines into Vietnam until our country did in fact (and this is true) have one of the five largest air forces in the world, with at one time over a thousand planes and nearly half that number of helicopters. Yet (so the critics say) our sense of twentieth-century technology was so poor that we could hardly keep a dozen planes in the air at the same time. Horrific stories have been printed of squadrons of planes grounded at Saigon for want of a spare sparkplug or gasket still unpacked in the vast storehouses at Bien Hoa, where the Americans at one stage shipped much of their material. Even the sternest critics, however, admit that, in the words of Joseph B. Treaster of *The New York Times*, "It was a young and enthusiastic air force with more spunk than the army." What, then, went wrong?

The most damaging fault was the American belief that all the United States had to do was create a Vietnamese air force in its own American image and it could be used to beat the North Vietnamese in the way that the American air force was used to beat the Germans in Europe. It was a philosophy that the Americans could never forget, and a policy which could never succeed in Vietnam, even though at times, when I was leading the air force, we were flying up to a thousand sorties a day.

The reason for the inevitable failure of the American approach lay in history. It went right back to the days when the French pulled out and started to train us. France, after World War II, was a poor nation but one that had always been proud of its skill in improvisation. So the French started our air force on a shoestring. We learned *everything* there was to know about flying. Equally important, the maintenance engineers were also taught *everything* about an airplane. Often there was only one engineer for each plane, and he had to be equally skillful at adjusting the hydraulic system or replacing a broken feed pipe or tracing a faulty electrical connection. And then, having sorted out the problems, he had nine times out of ten to improvise a solution. We had only a few planes in those days, but the men who worked all night long in the hangars to keep them flying were the salt of the skies, as good mechanics, as trustworthy, as hardworking, as painstaking as any you could find in the world.

Then the first American advisers arrived, and set to work to train a new breed of mechanic, based on exactly opposite theories to those practiced by the thrifty French. Soon the first mountain of spare parts arrived. And those spare parts were there to be *used*.

I shall always remember a tough but kindly American technical sergeant walking into a hangar, and his mouth dropping open as he saw a Vietnamese engineer scraping a sparkplug clean with his penknife.

"For Chrissake," he said half jokingly, "what the hell would happen to the American economy if everyone did that? Here, chuck it away. We've got a million more out there." When I saw the lavish—almost wasteful—use of spares I often related it to food piled high on American army plates, half of it to be thrown away because the portions were too large. Maybe it *was* good for the economy (for those who could afford it) but to us those plugs were as precious as rice is to a peasant.

The irony of this kind of wastage lies in the fact that for the time being it certainly was more efficient. No one can deny that, given the money and the production lines, the American system kept the planes going. War is an expensive business anyway, but time is more precious than money. In the old days it might have taken a French-trained mechanic days to trace and rectify an engine fault. But an American-trained engineer could reduce those days to hours merely by throwing the old engine away and winching a new one into place. Tighten a few nuts and bolts, clip in a few electric leads, and that plane is in the firing line right away. This procedure, however, was based on an American presence *remaining* in Vietnam.

But it was twenty years since the first French-trained mechanics tinkered with our first DC3s. These men were, by now, too old, too set, too thrifty to fit in with the U.S. pattern of strength through mass, nor had they been trained to handle the more sophisticated planes that we were receiving toward the end. In their place a new kind of aircraft maintenance crew was born, or rather trained, by the Americans. These new Vietnamese technicians despised their tinkering predecessors.

Now, as we faced defeat, came the crunch: not only an American pull-out but a river of spares that dwindled to a trickle, and finally into a dry river bed. When the American Congress voted "No more arms" the men who twenty years ago could have kept those last planes in the air by improvisation had been long forgotten. Their successors had never been trained for such an eventuality. They could put an engine in, because that is what the Americans had trained them to do—in the belief that there would always be engines to put into planes as long as the war lasted. But now there were no spare engines. And if you asked the new breed of mechanics to dig into the entrails of a plane and improvise, many of them hardly knew where to begin. To me it was a miracle that, even in the last two years of the war, when Vietnam was fighting alone, the air force was at times still providing hundreds of missions a day.

Despite all these problems, North Vietnam could have been stopped and, what is more, Nixon made it clear in Paris that they would be stopped if they infringed on the agreement. It was a basic promise of the Paris accord that any violations would be followed by terrible American retribution. I understand that Nixon privately warned the Communists that America, with its latest laser bomb, had a new capability that could destroy the North in hours.

At the beginning of 1974 the North Vietnamese decided on a classic Communist strategy: "Prod and if necessary withdraw." To test America's nerve, armed units from the North launched a carefully prepared conventional attack. The advance was small. The troops then waited for the American reaction. In Washington Nixon drafted a tough "We're going to get 'em" speech in late February, warning that he was prepared to bomb North Vietnam.

The speech was never delivered, for with the ides of March a bomb exploded much nearer home. The tightrope on which

Nixon had been precariously balancing snapped as the "Watergate Seven," including Attorney General Mitchell, were sent for trial.

Nixon was on the skids. And through the long hot summer before Nixon resigned, no one—but no one—in the United States gave a second thought to South Vietnam.

19

GRAHAM MARTIN:

Formula for a double cross

I returned to politics on March 27, 1975, after more than three years out of office, to launch an organization called the National Salvation Committee.

The decision was forced upon me. I thought I had given up politics, if only because Thieu's control was so all-embracing that effective opposition was impossible. But the military situation was growing desperate and anyone could see that unless something drastic was done, the war would be lost. More and more civilian groups were turning against Thieu, and I became more involved gradually as I returned at regular intervals to the house that I still kept at the Saigon air base.

The opposition grew but it lacked a leader. There were meetings almost daily of Catholics, Buddhists, and all the political factions, but their energies were dissipated by the absence of an alternative president.

Old friends from the air force came to my house seeking my support for action. One group of pilots actually sought my approval to bomb the palace and kill Thieu.

I had to tell them: "It is impossible. The enemy is outside Saigon and if we stage a coup we must achieve success within hours. We cannot afford to make a military attack that drags on or the Vietnamese will be fighting among themselves and the Communists will take advantage of the situation. It is better to start political pressures and hope that the Americans realize the whole country has turned against Thieu."

For Thieu would never have remained without the backing of the Americans, who wanted stability above all else. The tragedy is that if Ambassador Graham Martin had not backed Thieu he might have been deposed three months before the end came, in which case Vietnam might have survived.

In mid-March Tran Van Do, a former foreign minister, Bui Diem, the president's special emissary, and Tran Quoc Buu, a labor leader, visited Thieu on behalf of a group of moderates and told him bluntly that he no longer had the confidence of the people. He did nothing, so they came to see me.

I called a press conference in the Officers' Club at the air base, where I knew the police could not stop it. Thieu's intelligence service was as good as ever, though, and two days before it, trying to blunt my attack, he told Prime Minister Khiem to form a war cabinet in which anyone of anti-Communist views might serve. And on the eve of my meeting he broadcast, announcing a lowering of the age of conscription to seventeen, a ban on men of military age leaving the country, and closure of the country's nightclubs and race courses. None of these measures, nor all of them together, answered the needs of the country.

I gave my press conference. The National Salvation Committee was not a new name. A National Salvation Front had come into being after the Tet offensive of 1968, when Senator Tran Van Don brought together 2,000 representatives of political, religious, tribal, labor, professional, youth, and social organizations. Later it had been absorbed into an Alliance for Social Revolution and in 1969 Don had tried to turn it into a political party largely representing the interests of army veterans.

The title seemed apt in the 1975 situation. I demanded a government of national salvation, insisting that even if Thieu did not resign as president—and I could not see him doing that —he should delegate full powers to a government of new men —young men—with new policies.

We had four main goals: the first was to get rid of Thieu; the second to fight corruption; the third to provide an honest government; and the last, but not least, to stop the Communist advance.

I wanted Thieu to hand over power to a collective leadership that could rally the forces and the people. I saw myself as prime minister because I thought I was the most likely person to attract the necessary public support, though I anticipated devoting myself to the military task of averting defeat while others tackled the stabilizing of the economy and the political situation.

One of my main helpers in the National Salvation Committee was the Catholic priest Father Thanh, whose anticorruption movement was highly successful. Shortly after his first public appearance denouncing corruption, when he demanded Thieu's resignation, Father Thanh came to see me at my house on the base. He wished to associate himself with our party, and was of enormous help.

From our first broad base we started our political negotiations. We were realistic enough to accept some changes in our basic thinking. Six years previously we would never have thought of sitting down at talks with the Communists. Now we realized that a long-drawn-out war was impossible. But I felt, and so did my colleagues, that if we were to survive as a non-Communist political entity we could only operate from strength. We had to stop the Communist advance before the talking began. This we could not do without a new team, without voluntary support, without a new spirit. That was the real aim of the NSC. That is why Father Thanh came to me. He represented the poor but honest people, while I represented the military.

If only we had had time, if only the Americans had not stopped us, we might have done something. Even if we had lost Saigon, we still had the Mekong Delta. My plan was really to make Saigon a Stalingrad. All the women, all the children, all the old people would be evacuated. The only ones to remain in the city would be volunteers, but there would be half a million of us to defend our capital as the Russians had defended Stalingrad. We had plans to blow up all the bridges, to isolate Saigon. As I told Father Thanh, "That is worth dying for. A battle the world will always remember." An American correspondent said, "If you try to turn Saigon into a Stalingrad, thousands will die. Finally you will die. Do you really consider that to be a useful act?"

"I don't know," I replied. "All I do know is that I am a fighter. You mention the word Stalingrad. Do you realize after all these years people still know that name? That is enough for me. Stalingrad is one battle that changed the history of the world; maybe we could do the same thing."

Soon Thieu started to hit back, though he never dared to touch me. But he did arrest a number of people for plotting to overthrow him.

What we might have achieved is now difficult to estimate. Four days later hundreds of Buddhist monks from An Quang pagoda demonstrated against the new conscription regulations and demanded Thieu's resignation. They were led by Thich Tri Quang, who had been in the forefront in bringing about the downfall of Diem in 1963, but had, like me, been inactive for some years.

The tragedy is that we might have saved something out of the wreckage because I had one vital advantage over all other leaders in Vietnam. I am not referring to my policies or youth, but to the fact that I was, in those last weeks, the best-informed man on both the military and civilian situations as they fluctuated day by day. This is not an exaggeration, but was due to a chain of readily understandable circumstances. I was living on the air base, and had once commanded the air force. The Air Operations Center was the key to almost every military situation, either defense or attack. Inevitably men who had served with me, had on occasion been appointed by me, talked matters over, at times asked my advice. More and more information started flowing in. Almost instinctively—I certainly never asked for the information—officers brought me all the reports. Soon the Joint General Staff started bringing in their news. Then the politicians joined the stream of visitors to my house, so that I had an almost hour-by-hour report on everything that was going on in the country. In fact my house became a kind of sorting office, an unofficial headquarters.

Everyone demanded change, but until I formed the National

Salvation Committee the cries of frustration had lacked unity. As the country crumbled about us everyone knew there was only one slender hope of saving Vietnam: get rid of the enigmatic, brooding President Thieu, a man who would never give a firm "Yes" or "No." Even when he was American ambassador, Bunker once begged me to try to persuade Thieu to take a certain course, complaining, "The problem with Thieu is that he agrees to everything, but does nothing." Thieu always smiled—especially to the Americans—and never took any action.

Catholics, Buddhists, conflicting political parties staged daily demonstrations urging his removal. In Cholon hundreds of bets a day were laid on the date of his departure from office. But Thieu stayed, for he was embraced in the protective arms of the United States. We might regard Thieu as a traitor, but he was backed by Graham Martin. Martin was a Kissinger man and Kissinger was by now bored with Vietnam, and too involved in his latest highly publicized peace shuttle in the Middle East to bother with our fate.

Graham Martin stood obstinately in our path; a Nixon-appointed man, a Kissinger protégé, he was totally different from the man we had hoped would succeed Bunker, though when his appointment as ambassador was first announced toward the end of 1973, it had seemed a welcome change, for we needed a sterner American policy. The Kissinger-inspired cease-fire already began to look like a sellout, and Vietnam required a man to help warn the State Department to be firm with the Communists if they broke the agreement.

Martin, sixty-three-year-old son of a poor North Carolina preacher, had already done a stint as ambassador to Thailand, but he was conceited, a man incapable of changing his mind, and I believe he was directly responsible for the tragic refusal of Congress to give Vietnam its last aid request, because Martin was thoroughly distrusted and disliked in Washington. Many who had taken part in the peace talks—notably Philip Habib, head of the U.S. delegation—could not stand Martin. Many believed he was not sending truthful cables back to headquarters in Washington.

There were other factors. Martin attacked David Shipler of *The New York Times* in a 4,600-word cable to the State Department. Martin suggested that Shipler's reporting "might well be made available to the Columbia Graduate School of Journalism as a case study of propaganda under the guise of 'investigative reporting.'" Martin's cable to the State Department was leaked and became highly embarrassing to the United States government.

A few weeks later Martin was in trouble with a religious leader—in the person of George Webber, the anti-war president of the New York Theological Seminary, who visited Saigon. Martin asked Webber to appeal to the Communist delegation in Saigon to stop terrorist attacks. Webber apparently did not have time to see the Communists, and when he returned home to America a chilling package awaited him. It consisted of terrible photos of mutilated children, and it had been sent by Martin, who also wrote Webber, "You will have to live with the unresolvable doubt that, but for your decision not to call, these children might still be alive." That letter was also leaked.

When thirty-four-year-old Hoang Duc Nha, our American-trained information minister, warned Thieu that Martin was making empty promises, that he was in fact lying to the State Department, Martin had him fired in the fall of 1974. But Nha had been right, for when Martin's request for nearly $1.5 million in military aid was halved by Congress in the fiscal year 1974–75 Martin told Thieu blandly that there was no need to worry because most of the sum would be made up by an extra grant later. As all the world knows, Congress voted to stop aid entirely.

It is hard, looking back, to view the actions of either Martin or Thieu without a feeling of anger. For now the final Communist onslaught was upon us, and to me it was agony to watch helplessly as the stupidity mounted, for I *knew* the values of each leader, and was able to assess the strength and weakness of our army. After years as prime minister, I understood the psychology of each general, the capacity of each army unit. As chairman of the Military Council and vice president I had always kept in touch with the armed forces, and even during the last three years as a civilian, I had continued my visits to army units. So it was that during the last twenty-five days of Communist attack, I followed, hour by hour, the developments on the battlefields of Kontum, Ban Me Thuot, Danang, Nha Trang, Phan Rang, Phan Thiet, Xuan Loc, and finally Saigon.

The Communists began their massive attack with a small but significant operation, when guerrillas assaulted an outpost on National Highway 21 between Nha Trang and Ban Me Thuot. This outpost, the first one to fall, was barely forty miles from my farm in Khanh Duong. I was at the farm that day, and when I heard the news, I flew back to Saigon to warn army leaders that the move heralded a Communist plan to attack the Highlands region, and possibly Ban Me Thuot.

When General Timmes of the CIA came to see me, I asked him whether the Americans and Thieu realized that Ban Me Thuot was threatened. Both Timmes and General Cao Van Vien, head of the Joint General Staff, told me they were fully informed about Communist plans to take Ban Me Thuot. Vien added that he had been present at a meeting with Thieu, General Phan Van Phu, commander of Second Corps, and General Le Van Tuong, commander of the 23rd Division, defending Ban Me Thuot. Thieu warned Phu that the Communist 320th Division was moving southward to attack Ban Me Thuot. Phu assured everyone that he was completely aware of all developments, and Thieu then gave instructions to Phu and Tuong to reinforce Ban Me Thuot with more troops.

I mention this in some detail because it proves that the suggestion that our troops were caught by surprise at Ban Me Thuot is totally untrue. The Americans and Thieu knew about the Communist strategy months before they moved. In fact Ban Me Thuot was captured because General Phu hesitated. Despite Thieu's order to send more troops into Ban Me Thuot, Phu waited a week before implementing the order. Six hours before the Communists attacked, Phu had flown in only four hundred troops. Had Phu prepared seriously to defend Ban

Me Thuot, I am convinced the Communists would not have taken it. After all, the enemy attacked with only one division, and as it was, Ban Me Thuot held out for days, with one of my friends, the parachutist Colonel Vu The Quang, dying heroically. When surrounded by Communist tanks, Quang asked for air attack against them, but was told he was too close to the target. He insisted. The tanks were destroyed, but Colonel Quang's HQ also received a direct hit.

After Ban Me Thuot was lost, I had another meeting with General Vien, and suggested that the enemy line could be pierced from National Route 21, near my farm. I was certain that by concentrating artillery and air power, and two regiments of veteran paratroopers or Rangers, it would take only two days to reoccupy Ban Me Thuot. I volunteered to lead the attack, and General Vien agreed the plan was feasible. Alas, it was vetoed by President Thieu.

There can be no doubt that our military defeat was largely due to the dissension between the Joint General Staff and Thieu. Vien told me that he was so unhappy with the way Thieu rejected the advice of the Joint General Staff, and refused to consult with them, that he had tendered his resignation several times, especially after Thieu himself decided on all transfers and appointments of general officers. But Vien's requests to resign were curtly refused by Thieu. After the loss of Ban Me Thuot, Thieu held a meeting of generals in Camranh, where he ordered General Phu to withdraw from Kontum and Pleiku to the south and consolidate a defense line south of Ban Me Thuot, with the intention of recapturing the town. It was a tragic mistake. If we had brought in the Rangers plus tanks from north of Kontum and Pleiku, the Communist-held Ban Me Thuot would have been caught in a vise. Instead, Thieu's strategic error turned a tactical withdrawal into a rout and the eventual disintegration of our entire armed forces.

Soon the entire Second Army Corps was in full retreat from the Highlands, together with hundreds of thousands of refugees caught in the grip of confusion and chaos. It was to be the beginning of South Vietnam's last defeat.

By now, loss of confidence was sweeping our army, as infectious as a plague. (It was not helped by America's refusal to send aid.) With the Highlands gone, General Ngo Quang Truong pulled back his forces to defend Danang. Truong planned to concentrate troops at several coastal enclaves, but as soldiers watched their commanding officers—who had called on them to stay and fight—preparing for their families to escape, the men lost all sense of purpose. And, too, they could see hundreds of thousands of civilians fleeing in panic. Communists exacerbated the situation by infiltrating saboteurs, spreading rumors. Finally, Military Region I, containing the bravest men in the army, a marine division, an airborne division, the 1st Infantry Division, and the strongest armored and air forces of all South Vietnam, suffered an even more tragic defeat. The generals and officers fled to the sea.

Despite the fact that Martin tried to run the American embassy as a one-man show, my collated information was so vital in the last weeks that soon one member of the embassy was visiting me regularly to glean information. He was none other than General Timmes of the CIA, who wanted to report back all the latest situation reports to the embassy. I was delighted to help him. After a week of exhausting trips to my house along roads often blocked by demonstrations, Timmes made life a little easier: he had a private telephone line installed between the American embassy and my house on the base.

As the days ticked by and the news got worse, I thought about the possibilities of a coup, but reality said No. If a coup misfired, it would spark off hatred leading to rioting, and the only winners would be the Communists. Martin also made it very clear that if our National Salvation Committee took any steps to unseat Thieu, we would be in trouble.

The warning came in a roundabout fashion when the chief of the air force, General Minh (no relation to Big Minh), came to see me. I had originally appointed Minh to his job, and when we talked about the need for a change—in other words, getting rid of Thieu—he said, "You are still my boss, and I will follow you whatever you do. But let me warn you—if you decide to do something, be very careful, because otherwise they will kill you first."

"You are very honest with me," I replied, "but you must know more than you have told me. Can't you be more specific?"

"Martin is watching you," he replied. "The Americans have sent people to me to try to convince me not to work with you if you make any move. Martin's men have even tried to bribe me. They have told me that if I behave myself, even if we lose, they will get me and my family out and take care of us for the rest of our lives."

Within days the warning was brought home in more direct fashion, when one of my pilots burst into my room, puffing and blowing as he blurted out an extraordinary story. Seeing a suspicious-looking character walking inside the base perimeter, he challenged him, asked who he was. The man bolted. The pilot gave chase, brought the man down with a football tackle, only to find that he *did* have a proper pass.

"Then why did you run?" asked my pilot, who was so suspicious that he marched the man to the guardroom. The special security pass was in order, but something was wrong somewhere.

"Where is the man?" I asked.

"Outside."

"Good for you. Bring him in."

After interrogation the man admitted, "Many of us are for you, Marshal, but we work for General Quang and he sent us here. I can't do anything—I have a wife and kids."

I took a note of their address and promised to go and get them and keep them safely on the base. Then the man poured out his story. General Quang was at the bottom of a plot to assassinate me if I became too dangerous.

Dang Van Quang was the man I had dismissed for corruption. Thieu had reinstated him and now he was special adviser to the president on security. Somehow he had obtained fifteen special passes normally issued to the security guards, and had given them to men assigned to kill me, at a time when the

Communists were racing toward the capital and security was vital.

"We were told to wait for orders," the would-be assassin told me, "but I beg you to remain in your house. If you go out, you could be killed."

We mounted a full-scale "attack," and we found all of the assassins. We made no announcements, but kept them on the base so that Quang would be lulled into a false sense of optimism.

Yet, even though the Communists were approaching, nothing could be done to save the country while Thieu was in power. But if Thieu went, I believed that we could make a last stand against the Communists. I knew from my daily information reports that we had reserves of ammunition, though we had lost great stores at Danang. We still had large reserves of manpower, also, and though it was easy for the world to sneer at "Vietnamese cowards," I knew I could trust those men, despite what had happened. I knew how morale can snap when leadership is bad, as ours was, but I was convinced that under the right leaders, inspired by patriotism, the very men who panicked and fled from Danang would fight to the death. I hoped and prayed that I might be the man chosen by destiny to provide that inspiration, and to prove to the world that Vietnamese soldiers—and their commanding officers—were prepared to die to defend their country's flag and honor.

But first, Thieu had to go, and at times I almost despaired. Then came the bombshell. One morning General Timmes phoned and asked if he could come and see me that afternoon, adding in a casual voice, "Would you mind if I bring with me"—and I will always remember the words—"a high authority?"

"Not at all," I replied, thinking that perhaps the top brass of the CIA had arrived in Saigon and wished to see me.

Timmes arrived exactly on time at 3 P.M.—and who should be with him but Ambassador Martin. I had not seen Martin for some time and I was appalled at the physical change in the man who now stood in the doorway of my house. Still suffering from the aftereffects of pneumonia, he seemed to have shriveled. His eyes were sunken and red-rimmed. He still looked arrogant and, above all, conceited—a trait that his first words did nothing to belie. They were truly astonishing.

"You must be surprised to see a man like me at your house," he said condescendingly. He apparently regarded it as an honor for a diplomat on the verge of retirement to visit a young man who had, after all, been prime minister. He must have seen my reaction—one of pity rather than anger—for as I offered the two men tea, Martin told me that he had once been a pilot. Perhaps he was trying to break the ice. At any rate we did talk for two hours, the first time we had ever thrashed out the problems facing Vietnam, and I found him, if not sympathetic, at least realistic—or so I thought.

When he asked me about Thieu I told him, "All my committee wants is for Thieu to resign, and to replace him with a strong, effective government to organize the fight against the Communists."

He was probing, for he asked me guardedly, "This is a hypothetical question, Marshal, but if you were able to form a new government, how would you treat Thieu?"

It was an odd question. I replied truthfully, "I hate him, and I know that he is having a bad influence on the fate of our country, but I have no spirit of revenge against a man like Thieu. If I were to take over, I would let him go. In fact, to be truthful, it is up to the people to judge Thieu and his government. It would never be my problem. All I want is the authority to organize—and then to fight."

Martin even went so far as to inquire if I had given any thought to the problems of forming a new government, and I told him I had, naming names. "If we have the sort of government I want," I added, "I could organize effective resistance in a matter of days. But we can't afford any delay. Every day is a day nearer defeat."

"You talk about fighting," said Martin, "but there's a big difference between talking and acting. I know you are extremely well informed—but what would you fight with? Think of the losses you sustained at Danang alone."

"Defeats like Danang may sound bad," I explained, "and

we certainly lost a huge stockpile there, but my information
is that we have three months' supplies of weapons and ammunition. I know that we could hold out—not forever, but long
enough to create a new climate, so that we could be in a
stronger position when it comes to talking peace."

"Then *how?*" he asked. Timmes had brought along a map
and we spread it out on the floor. I drew a line across it from
Nha Trang, just north of Camranh Bay, roughly the 13th
parallel.

"We've got to stop the advance here. . . ." I followed the line
with my pencil. "If we can hold the enemy here, and at the
same time have a new, strong government team, a new atmosphere, I will guarantee you the support of the entire nation.
Then we will be in a position of strength to start talks with the
enemy."

"Will the men fight?" he asked.

"Of course they will," I assured him, telling him of the
officers from Danang who had arrived at my house thirsting for
revenge, adding that despite the press reports the Vietnamese
were not cowards. "Anyway," I asked, "what is the alternative?"

At the end of two hours Martin rose to go. "I am inclined to
think you are right," he said. He did not actually promise that
he would support me. But he did indicate that Thieu must go.
And he *had* asked me what sort of men I would put in any
new government. As he reached the door, he added, "It's not
easy, you know. Give me a few days—then we'll see what we
can arrange."

I had kept only one item of information from Martin: that
our committee had made tentative plans involving the air
force, paratroopers, and Special Forces to stage a last-minute
coup against Thieu if necessary, though I always hoped it
would not be necessary. Now, however, all was changed.

Elated, I told the members of my immediate staff the news,
adding, "The first thing we must do now is to call off the
projected coup."

Like a cold shower one of my aides warned me, "I don't trust
Martin. I think he could be double-crossing us." I doubted it,

but the aide said he believed Martin had merely come to lull us into inaction. "Why should he suddenly come to see you?" he asked. "What a simple way for him to stop any possible coup. Why should we have a coup when the American ambassador is behind us?"

Another aide suggested that Martin had visited me at the express request of Thieu, to sound out the strength of our movement. It seemed very devious, and I hated to be suspicious—yet I did know that Thieu's fear of assassination gnawed so deeply that he slept in a different house each night. But I had to give Martin the benefit of the doubt. He had certainly *seemed* sincere. We decided to wait for the American embassy to take action, even though the news was getting worse. One after another the coastal cities were falling, leaving Saigon wide open.

By April 20 my information was that fifteen North Vietnamese divisions—roughly 150,000 men—were closing in around the outer ring of Saigon's defenses. Other units were edging slowly along Route 1 toward Bien Hoa, our second-largest air base. Three more Communist divisions had crossed the border from Cambodia—the three I had hoped to destroy before the Americans refused permission—to take part in the final assault.

In Xuan Loc, northeast of Saigon, our troops had been holding out heroically for nearly two weeks against fearful odds, and at least my private intelligence grapevine helped to kill some of the attackers when they gave me the information that we actually had on Vietnamese soil a few five-ton bombs that had never been used. Nothing so large and destructive had been sent to Vietnam before, but there were two problems: we had no bomb racks big enough to carry them, and they could be employed only on written orders from the Joint General Staff.

Colonel Vu Van Uoc, chief of the Air Operations Center, who was in daily contact with me, suggested developing a new bomb rack on our old C30 planes. Someone high up said it could not be done. I telephoned a contact and got the decision reversed, and working throughout the night with Vietnamese maintenance men, we built a new bomb rack and dropped our first bomb on Xuan Loc. The destruction was so enormous that for three days there was no fighting. The North Vietnamese were terrified of further destruction.

We wanted to use more bombs, but each time we needed written permission from the Vietnamese General Staff, and Uoc complained that when he had perfect targets he could not get permission. Finally I called a friend on the General Staff and told him what was happening, stressing that time was all-important. How typical of those last confused days that nobody would give anyone an order until finally a civilian like myself made a phone call. My friend said, "No problem. Use the bombs when you need to."

It did not change the outcome of the war, but perhaps some of us found a modest sense of achievement, of satisfaction, in being able to hit back at the hated enemy, even if it was now too late. For by now the end was rushing upon us.

20

SAIGON:

The final agony

We had shelved the idea of a coup to depose President Thieu, trusting the American ambassador, but as the hours ticked by, our first nagging impatience for action began to turn into qualms of doubt. My "hot line" telephone to the American embassy had become strangely silent. The daily phone calls from Timmes—always so friendly, always so encouraging—had unaccountably dried up. I came under more and more pressure from my colleagues on the National Salvation Committee to take drastic action. Finally I could delay no longer. I picked up the phone and asked Timmes bluntly, "What's happening?"

He was not exactly evasive, but he seemed to hesitate. It is not always easy (or fair) to form a conclusion from a phone talk, but I had the impression that he was embarrassed.

"For the moment our hands are tied," he said. "It's very difficult, very delicate. Just hang on until we let you know." It was clear that something funny was going on, especially when I learned that Martin's behavior was becoming nothing short of bizarre. More and more he was playing the role of an arrogant Caesar. While Washington urged him to prepare for a full-scale evacuation, he apparently disregarded their orders because he felt that a too-hasty evacuation program would damage the dignity of the United States and his own personal dignity.

How the Americans treated their own people in Saigon was their affair, but there were hundreds of Vietnamese workers on the United States payroll who would be marked for certain death if Saigon fell. They had all been promised a ticket to safety. Martin had boasted, "If Americans have to go, I will take a million Vietnamese with me."

Well, while Washington told him to do just this in cables that he ignored, I could see the result for myself on the air base. Scores of big U.S. transport planes flew in past my windows every day, loaded with precious supplies—but nearly all flew back half empty, when they could have taken a far more precious cargo to safety.

Martin did try to persuade Phan Quang Dan, deputy prime minister, to allow orphans to be evacuated, but this was for propaganda, for Martin wrote in a letter to Dan that "this evacuation . . . will create a shift in American public opinion in favor of Vietnam," explaining that, once in America, the children would appear on TV and "the effect would be tremendous."

In fact Martin was hoping to persuade Congress to reverse its veto on arms aid to Vietnam, and he backed his plan up with a never-ending stream of photographs of atrocities and inspired stories calculated to wring the hearts of American people, at the same time as he was assuring all of us, "Be calm. Saigon is in no danger."

Even more incredible, at this critical moment he ordered embassy officials to compile a detailed study of the Vietnamese government information service. The man was not only stupid. He was mad.

Suddenly contacts inside the government told me on my private grapevine that Thieu was on the point of being ordered to resign. "There's no doubt about it," one told me, "all they're doing now is trying to find a formula to save everyone's face."

I knew my informant was telling the truth—but then, why didn't Martin telephone me to prepare the National Salvation Committee for action? As suspicion started to bite deeper, I suggested that we look again at our plans for a coup against Thieu. And it was because of this plan that I finally learned of Martin's double cross. Unexpectedly Timmes arrived at my house, and almost casually dropped a name that gave me the first clue.

"Is it true," he asked me, "that some of the general officers from the North—men like you—are plotting a coup?" My immediate reaction was that there must have been a leak, but before I had time to say a word, Timmes added an extraordinary sentence, a few words that absolved me from the decision of whether or not to lie.

"I mean a move against Big Minh."

I was flabbergasted. After all, Big Minh had been out of power for a long time. I blurted out, "I've heard nothing—but why Minh? He's not the president. Why should anyone make a move against a man who's not in power?"

Timmes replied, "Well, Marshal, I think I ought to tell you that if you *do* make a move against Big Minh, Washington and Hanoi will blame you for anything that happens afterward."

That was the split second when I realized that Martin had been quietly using the National Salvation Committee as a blind while he was planning to kick out Thieu, presumably to replace him with Big Minh as the man to negotiate with the Communists.

More in horror than in anger I said to Timmes, "If Big Minh becomes president, there will be a total collapse of Vietnam in twenty-four hours. Why should the Communists talk with Big Minh? He's not popular, and he never will be."

As Timmes left, I wondered if the Americans were just naïve enough to believe that Big Minh could deal with the Communists. Yet Martin was not naïve. Nor was Kissinger. Perhaps this incredible move was part of a carefully defined policy. Realizing that the end had come—though I could not believe it even then—perhaps the United States had decided to abandon us, and by putting in a man without any intellectual capabilities, to throw the last blame onto us instead of taking their share. There is no doubt that the choice of Big Minh was dictated by Martin.

But Big Minh did not become president—not for a few days. Instead, something quite unforeseen happened. Martin forced Thieu to go, but with some bizarre thought of obeying the laws of protocol, he replaced him with the vice president.

I shall never forget the moment when fifty-two-year-old

Thieu told the people of Vietnam that he had been forced out of office. Two hundred friends and followers were jammed in my house to listen to the pathetic hour-long speech by the man Martin had backed, the man who had allowed the Reds to reach the outskirts of the capital. We could hear the gunfire as we listened and watched.

I was ashamed. Ashamed that any Vietnamese leader could behave as Thieu behaved in his speech. Looking at the small TV screen, at Thieu in an open-necked bush shirt, my mind flashed back to the day Johnson agreed to my request to install television in Vietnam. I felt almost sorry we had ever discussed the matter of TV as Thieu started to blame the United States for its lack of resolve. In a tirade against those who had kept him in office, he accused America of not fulfilling its obligations.

Dr. Kissinger, he said, had tricked him into signing the Paris peace agreement and had then gone back on his word by refusing to send military aid to South Vietnam. We had lost because the United States failed to re-supply the army and send aid. "You ran away and left us to do the job that you could not do. We have nothing and you want us to achieve where you failed," he accused the Americans angrily. "At the time of the peace agreement the United States agreed to replace equipment on a one-for-one basis. But the United States did not keep its word. Is America's word reliable these days?"

Then came the surprise. Thieu was succeeded by the vice president, seventy-one-year-old Tran Van Huong; dear old Huong, the ex-schoolmaster, who had given me such a handsome wedding gift of 200,000 piastres. By now his eyesight was so bad that he could hardly read. When Huong became president I could only assume that Big Minh was waiting in the wings.

There followed a week of terror and confusion. Huong was a nonentity. Nothing was done to stem the onward surge of the enemy. By April 26 the Communists had cut Saigon off from its main source of food, and its only remaining port, Vung Tau, forty-five miles southeast of the capital. Twice they had bom-

barded the heart of Saigon, as a foretaste of things to come if
we did not capitulate.

Desperate, I determined to make one last effort, by asking
Huong to appoint me head of the armed forces. All of us
wanted to fight, yet nothing could be done without backing.
Heroics had nothing to do with it. Courage was immaterial.
You cannot fly planes unless you plan and work as a team with
more men on the ground than in the air. To fight, even for a
brief time, we needed to fight "officially." I decided to drive to
the presidential palace, in Saigon, and it took me over an hour
to reach the heart of the capital. I was appalled at what I saw,
the ugly and yet unreal atmosphere. In the way that imminent
tragedy sometimes makes people light-headed, there seemed
to be no sense of doom, but rather one of nervous hilarity: the
determined cheerfulness of a frightened patient before he is
wheeled into the operating theater.

Hoping to find an American senior officer and learn the
latest news, I dropped by Saigon's famous *Cercle Sportif*, a
tennis and swimming club near the palace dating from colonial
times, but for the past decade a favorite haunt of American top
brass. No longer. The change was so startling that I might have
stepped twenty years back in time. No Americans and no
pretty Vietnamese girls were suntanning themselves by the
pool as usual. Instead the *Cercle Sportif* was French again.
Martin had arranged with the French ambassador, Jean-Paul
Merillon, to mediate between North and South when necessary. With this "power," the first thing the French did was to
take back their beloved *Cercle Sportif*. There they were, ordering Pernod and vermouth cassis, delighted, unable to believe
that the past they thought had gone forever had caught up
with them.

But for the rest of Saigon there was nothing but tears and
terror. I found evidence of looting in the market, near the
Botanical Gardens, and also from an American PX which had
either been abandoned or broken into, I never found out which.
A mob was tearing away barbed-wire defenses. Sweating men
lugged refrigerators in tri-shaws; others carried boxes of food,

cartons of cigarettes, even chewing gum. On the side of the road was a mound of soap flakes in boxes. Presumably no one considered them useful. I saw one tri-shaw filled with bottles that at first I could not recognize. One dropped off and as it nearly hit my jeep, I jammed on the brakes and picked the bottle up. It contained the red marinated cherries Americans use in cocktails. Kids darted in and out among their elders for packets of cigarettes or chewing gum as the older people worked frantically removing (presumably to hoard against the future) anything they could lay their hands on: packages of frozen meat, sweets, bars of chocolate.

Down the street I saw a soldier roll up his sleeves and proudly display his arms to a friend. He had wristwatches strapped all the way up to both elbows. As I turned a corner, and had to stop for a moment, I saw a kid sitting in the back of a tri-shaw. He had what looked like an expensive camera slung around his neck, but he also had something else—a revolver and a sub-machine gun. By the American embassy looters were taking away carpets, porcelain bathtubs, sofas, chairs, even filing cabinets.

The stench was everywhere—a compound of river smells, the whiff of spices, uncleaned open drains, dried fish, the stink of smashed cases of whiskey.

Saigon was always a noisy city but never as raucous as now, with the sheets crowded, people's voices raised, tired men loping along with heavy burdens faster than usual in the heat, and as a background to everything, like a radio turned low, a sound like sullen thunder—the thunder of the guns.

As soon as I reached the presidential palace, I was taken in to see President Huong and I begged him, "Name me commander of the armed forces, Sir. Give me an official post so that I can uphold the honor of Vietnam."

Huong was an old man waiting for the grave, and he answered in his high-pitched, faltering voice, "I can't do it. A man who has become vice president and prime minister can't suddenly become the commander of the armed forces. It is not possible, but perhaps in a few days I might be able to appoint you my special assistant for military affairs."

"But you can't wait a few days," I cried. "I don't care about protocol. I want to lead the forces right now."

He shook his head—and that meant that none of us could fight. The war was in effect over, because none of my brave pilots could fly when nobody was there to give orders to back them up. And once the Joint General Staff senses that the end is coming, nobody will ever give anyone any orders.

Huong lasted a week as president. Then Martin, having observed the niceties of diplomacy by allowing the vice president to step up (since there had been no election), now felt the time had come to install his protégé, Big Minh. It was decided to replace Huong on April 28, and on the 27th the fifty-nine-year-old Big Minh was asking both houses of the National Assembly for their formal approval, when the Communists gave a demonstration of their disapproval—by flying three jets captured from us in the North over the presidential palace, clearly indicating that they were unwilling to talk with Big Minh, but would take Saigon by force.

That was the night I talked to Von Marbod of the American Defense Department and begged him to help us to fight in the Mekong Delta—a request that was refused. The next morning my wife, Mai, and our children left for Honolulu on the last U.S. military plane to leave the base. She had twenty minutes to pack a suitcase after breakfast, and I was not even there to say farewell.

At three o'clock that afternoon the same pilot who had warned me of the assassins who had infiltrated the base on General Quang's orders came in with another piece of startling news. Thieu had, as we knew, bolted, but in the rush to run away he had forgotten all about Quang, his partner in crime.

"Quang's at the headquarters of the General Staff," said the pilot, "and I'm told he's absolutely furious. Thieu promised him a ride, then left without telling him."

A junior officer cried, "Can we go and arrest him, Sir—and execute him?"

"Go ahead and arrest him," I said, "but execution—no. That can come only after a proper trial."

Fate allowed Quang to get away. As the young officer and a friend were jumping into a jeep to drive the half mile to headquarters, two Communist planes swept down and bombed the base heavily. The officers were unable to get out and Quang was never seen in Saigon again. I understand he is now living in Canada.

Those two planes signaled the start of a concentrated offensive on the airfield. The Communists knew that once the airfield fell, Saigon was doomed. The first heavy bomb fell three hundred yards from my house. By now nearly four hundred people were congregated there or in the grounds surrounding it—military families who had been hoping for seats on a plane, some deciding to sleep in the office or in nearby buildings at night. It was like a refugee camp. As the first bombs shook the house, one pilot ran into my living room crying, "I am going to scramble."

I shouted, "I agree, go ahead!"

He rushed to the nearest fighter-bomber. I jumped into a jeep with a major and drove to the airstrip to see the extent of the damage. The base was uncanny, silent, deserted, in stark contrast to its normal busy life. Everyone had darted for shelter, and our jeep was the only moving object in sight. The Communist pilots must have spotted us, for the planes above wheeled around almost lazily, and then started strafing us. I could see the flashes of the guns aiming at the jeep as we jumped into a hole.

Scores of Vietnamese planes were destroyed on the ground. The electricity was cut off. We had no more communication with Joint General Staff headquarters and everyone in the house had to eat by candlelight.

About 9:30 P.M., the Communists started mortar and rocket fire, and by 11 P.M. I could stand the inaction no longer.

"Let's go up," I said to a couple of pilots and a navigator. We rushed out to my helicopter, took off and circled around. There were fires everywhere, the flames licking their way almost up to the perimeter of the base, and we could pick out the main Communist attacking positions easily because when they heard the noise of my helicopter they opened fire.

The biggest rocket battery seemed to be near the radio station. It was impossible to scramble any planes on the bombed and pitted runways of the airfield, but from the air I managed to contact Can Tho air base in the Mekong Delta and they loaded up four planes with 750-pound bombs. There was no time for code names when the planes arrived. I just yelled into the radio, "This is Marshal Ky, find the rocket position, then go in and destroy it."

As they moved into position, I watched from the helicopter, guiding them a little to the left, a little to the right, until they were dead on target. They destroyed the biggest bank of rockets.

When I was short of gas, I managed to refuel at the Shell depot in Nha Be, outside the city. Dozens of planes were lining up for gas. By now everyone was waiting for the end. It was strange watching old friends—pilots and navigators who had fought with me for years. Most had lost contact with their commands, and looked to me for guidance. I told those whose ammo had run out to refuel and fly back to Can Tho. Those whose choppers were armed turned back to Saigon, to drop their last bomb and fire their last bullet on an enemy which by now had advanced to the fences of Tan Son Nhut, my air base. Then they, too, would head back for the delta.

I flew back to Air Force Command Headquarters at Tan Son Nhut. It was utter confusion. The entire air force command, consisting of about a hundred generals, colonels, and majors, were grouped in the commander's office. I noticed some army generals too. The air force commander told me the Americans had ordered all F5 aircraft to be evacuated to Thailand or the Philippines. The air force commanding staff were to wait in the office for instructions from the Americans who would evacuate them.

Soon after dawn on the 29th the Communists started pounding the runway of the air base with their big Russian 130mm guns. Within minutes thick, oily smoke spread into a huge cloud as the enemy scored a direct hit on the main fuel depot. Several planes on the ground exploded in gigantic orange flashes, and there could be no doubt that the final offensive had opened. The Communists certainly knew that if they could destroy the air base there would be very little left of Saigon.

Still I waited in my house, even when I began to hear the spatter of machine-gun bullets—and that sounded as though the enemy was in a cemetery about half a mile away. As I was debating what to do, a car drew up at the gate. To my astonishment the Stars and Stripes fluttered on its mast, and out stepped Ambassador Martin. At first I assumed he was coming to see me, but of course that could not be possible, for he had no idea where I was. I heard later that it had taken him two hours to make the journey from the embassy and he had driven to the airfield with General Homer Smith because he could not believe it was now impossible to land planes at the base—which meant that the Americans could no longer organize a large-scale evacuation, but would have to carry people out of Vietnam in helicopters, making it impossible for Martin to keep his promise that all Vietnamese connected with the embassy would be evacuated.

Martin stayed only a few minutes and I can imagine his despair after driving around the airfield in a jeep and seeing that it was unserviceable. Then he and General Smith climbed back into his car.

However desperate the situation, I still clung to some hope. Climbing into my chopper I headed for the Joint General Staff headquarters. Perhaps I could make contact with other units, and perhaps urge them to reorganize their ranks to fight. But at JGS, I was told that the chief of staff had resigned and left Vietnam two days previously. The compound, normally filled with thousands of officers and soldiers, was almost deserted. I went up to the office of the chief of staff, and found it occupied by Lieutenant General Don Van Khuyen, acting chief of staff. I tried in vain to contact the navy and other units. Poor General Khuyen! He was alone and helpless. At 11:30 A.M., looking out over Saigon, I could see Air America planes filling up the sky. That meant the evacuation of Americans and Vietnamese government officials had started.

This was the moment when I realized all hope had gone. I called the Air Force Command again. The staff had moved to the U.S. defense attaché office and were being evacuated. I decided to leave, too. As I walked down the stairs, I met General Truong, former commander of Military Region I. "What are you doing here?" I asked him. Truong replied, "I don't know what to do any more." His family had left several days previously, so I told him, "Come along with me, then." I collected a dozen or so flyers, and we all piled aboard my helicopter as I started the motors whirring. I had hardly time to glance back at my house, where so much had happened, where the youngsters had been laughing only the previous morning, before we were over the city looking down on the streets alive with scurrying figures, the orange flames of fires dotting the picture. It all passed quickly—my last sight of beloved Saigon—as we headed out toward the sea. Every size and shape of vessel, from puny rowboats to carriers, seemed to fill the blue waters. Switching my radio on to a rescue emergency frequency, I made crackling contact with the U.S. carrier *Midway*, lying just off the coast. Willing voices guided me down to the deck.

The commander of the *Midway* was an old friend, Admiral Harris, who years previously I had decorated for his bravery and help to Vietnam, and he came forward to greet me, shook hands, and started to ask, "How are you?" But then he saw my face and left the sentence unfinished. Try as I could, it was hard to hold back the tears; very touchingly the admiral left me alone for a quarter of an hour before flying me in a helicopter to the U.S. command ship, the *Blue Ridge*.

Just before I boarded the chopper, I realized I had one last thing to do. I went back to my own helicopter, unbuckled my revolver, and laid it on the pilot's seat. It suddenly occurred to me that as the guest of another country I might have to hand in my gun, and I had visions of the manner in which a defeated commander hands over the sword. The situation was not quite analogous, but nonetheless I wanted to avoid the symbolic gesture.

I hate to sound ungrateful, but the initial hospitality on the *Blue Ridge* was rather different from that on the *Midway*.

When fourteen of us—all high-ranking officers—stepped out of the helicopter, the first words of welcome by an officious American colonel were a shout, "All of you, come here." He directed us to a table and asked, "Have you any objections to being searched?"

Halfway through this procedure somebody whispered to him. The colonel said to me in a low voice, "You, please come with me." He took me to his cabin and asked, "Where do you come from—Saigon?" I nodded. Finally he blurted out, "Are you Mr. Ky?" I nodded again.

Later that night, after I had been to see the commanding officer, the colonel came to apologize, and I told him that I fully appreciated the confusion, even suspicion, everywhere. But I could not forbear to add, "I understand that you might be suspicious, but after all, we have *all* sacrificed everything in this war. We may have lost, but we are not the *only* losers—you Americans have lost, too. What I can't understand is—why did you have to treat the officers who were with me the way you did? After all, we have been comrades in arms. We are not Communists, you know."

Martin also arrived on the *Blue Ridge*. He had bolted so swiftly from the American embassy that he had even left behind his photograph of Nixon. It was signed: "For all your great work in Indochina." With Martin came the reporters, who quickly asked me for a press conference. Martin sent his press officer to my cabin to try to persuade me not to hold one, but the persuasion was unnecessary. I had no desire to talk to anybody.

That night, for the first time in years, I took a sleeping pill. I remember thinking, as I asked for some tablets, that the medical officer would probably give me a small bottle. But he must have wondered if my dejection was potentially suicidal, for the doctor carefully handed me one pill and a glass of water, then waited and watched as I took it. I was not feeling suicidal, though perhaps occasionally the next day when I looked down at the sea from the huge height of the decks, with the coast of Vietnam in the distance, it did cross my mind that all you had to do was jump in and everything would be finished.

What I found so hard to realize was the speed with which the final explosion had erupted. Of course the news of the previous weeks had been grim, but less than a week previously, I had been begging the government to let me carry on the fight from the Mekong Delta, not in order to win a war—we had lost too much for that—but to be able to negotiate from a position of strength. Even a week ago it had seemed impossible that the end could come so swiftly.

Graham Martin and I did not talk to each other. Perhaps both of us were thinking of the Vietnamese members of the American embassy who had been left behind, even the firemen who had worked around the clock protecting the last helicopters to land at the embassy. Perhaps he was thinking of his promise, as the patient embassy workers, unable to believe that any American would break his word, waited for their turn to escape. For had not Martin said, "I will be the last man to leave this embassy. You have my solemn word on that."

Even when I saw him, a blue bathrobe over his shoulders, his eyes sunken, standing near a hatch on deck, I did not approach him. He was chewing an apple. Was he thinking of the many Vietnamese embassy workers left behind?

One of the workers who did get away appeared near him, and Martin muttered a few words. The man walked away. He was Martin's personal servant, and he was leading the ambassador's poodle, taking it for a "constitutional."

All the bustle and noise of a big ship suddenly subsided as a voice on the vessel's public address system boomed the famous navy "Now hear this. . . ." Then came the voice of the ship's chaplain.

"Men," he said, "you have delivered these latest children of Israel. Now I want you to pray for Vietnam, and then I want you all to relax and have a little fun."

INDEX